Comparative Research Study between Traditional and Online Modes of Education

Author: Durollari

Co-Author: Glasner

Table of Contents:

Abstract

This study uses a comparative research experiment to evaluate the differences between learning performance of traditional face-to-face modes of education with technology driven online distance education. This research study will investigate if there is a difference in academic performance between traditional modes of education and online delivery modes of education by evaluating final examination scores. A population of over 2,000 graduate level students, spanning a four-year period was used for data gathering and comparative analysis. This research will attempt to produce a comparison of the examination results between different delivery modes of study each year as well as between different classes over a 4-year period. Although it is believed that traditional mode students should be able to outperform their counterparts by scoring higher on final examinations and overall better performance records. This research will attempt to answer many of the questions concerning the perceived differences between traditional and online students.

Comparative Research Study between Traditional and Online Modes of Education

The education system throughout many parts of the world is still clinging to old fashioned modes of delivering education to the masses. Technology is outpacing these powerful institutions, and, in many cases, they have been forced to adopt, although at a slow to moderate pace. The current polices in education do not take into consideration the global dynamics and challenges faced by higher costs of energy and ever-changing needs of the people they are supposed to serve, the students. The average individual has very little input or control over their education, while being stuck in a slow evolving system based on old paradigms. The education system should be a collective effort between students, educators, and political figures to create the best possible system using the latest scientific teaching methods that works for everyone.

Politicizing the education system has placed strict guidelines on educators on what and how they teach, thus restricting creativity and real learning to take place. Technology is the key to solving many of today's social and educational issues; the problem is that technology is closely shrouded in secrecy by a few, leaving the majority at a technological disadvantage.

Society on whole needs to base decisions on logic and scientific evidence that is rooted in faith to address the real causes to educational system failures, or otherwise individuals and institutions will always be destined to repeat their mistakes. The political, social, and educational systems have served society well up to this point in history, but it does not address current needs or guarantee success for the future. Every individual need to actively get involved to discover new approaches towards fixing today's deficiencies; people can no longer keep on doing the same old, because the world is ever evolving and changing at a rapid pace. The future will require people will to be more innovative and highly trained in the sciences and technology, with the goal of developing better and smarter systems in the interest of society.

The social system should allow the smartest and best people involved in their process to come up with a sound and lasting solution and not only look towards our politicians for answers. Thinkers with personalities that work on the edges or frays of the society should be rewarded instead of being pushed aside and labeled as outcasts. It takes out of the box thinkers working outside the norm to create and discover new ideas or come up with smarter and different ways of doing things.

Technological advances have paved the way for delivering large amounts of data to users on demand, opening a new era on how people interact and learn. The purpose of this research study is to compare student performance between traditional learning environments and distance learning modes. This research study examines and compares the grade point averages between two different delivery modes of study.

The population under study will be required to complete final examinations in order to compare the differences in scores in the three factors consisting of courses that measure subject categories of theoretical, technical, and mathematical and then investigating the differences between the two factors of delivery modes of education, both traditional and online. The null hypothesis for this study states that there is no statistically significant difference in academic performance between traditional modes of education and online delivery modes of education after evaluating final examination scores.

The Problem Statement

Educators and students have been interested in decades in comparing the performance of students in technology driven distance learning courses and attending live lectures on campus. With the convenience of attending online classes many wonder if they are getting their monies worth in receiving a quality education. Another concern with online education is the lack of interaction between students and teachers as compared to live face-to-face lecture traditional schools offer.

This case study provided the opportunity to investigate the impact of online education on society while choosing the appropriate statistical methods to satisfy the question proposed in this study. The variables used in this experiment consisted of independent variables of traditional and online education and the dependent variable of students' grade point averages. The results of the statistical tests are significant in indicating differences between the scores of students in traditional classes with their counterparts of online students.

It is important to get a total number of students under the study along with using an equal grading scale. The statistical mean scores between the traditional and online students will need to be compared for any deviation between the groups.

The results will signify if there are differences in performance between traditional and online students. Finally, it is important to see if the research failed to reject the null hypotheses of disproving that there is no statistically significant difference between the performance of traditional and online students.

The Purpose of the Study

The main purpose of this research study is to differentiate college student performance while attending traditional classes on campus while compare them to students enrolled in distance learning online courses. This research will attempt to answer the question of which group of students will have higher grade point average. The aim of the research is to use student test results as a gauge to measure teaching and curriculum effectiveness between both groups, traditional and online.

The debate continues with many questioning the effectives of the online programs and whether its promise to equal traditional courses taught on campus. Online classes continue to gain momentum and are very popular amongst working adults and students that have a difficulty getting to campus facilities. The online schooling argument continues with many questioning the effectiveness or if the learning experience has been fulfilled as compared with face-to-face lectures taught on campus by live professors. Some studies suggest that it may not make a difference in student performance or learning. The major concern to online education is the effectiveness of this mode of education when dealing with more advanced courses in science and technology that require lab work and experimentation.

While some support the idea that some individuals will be less likely intrinsically motivated to learn when subjected to the freedom of online education has to offer. There is no doubt that it takes a more mature and self-motivated individuals to attend online courses. The biggest concern with online education is that many teachers feel less in control of the learning environment, while delegating responsible to students for their own learning. Future research is required to address the underlying issues involved in teacher-student interaction as it relates to student and learning in the traditional and online environment.

The Hypotheses and Research Questions

This comparative research study examines the differences in learning performance between traditional brick-and-mortar modes of education and technology driven online distance education, while evaluating academic examination results. The hypothesis for this research states that this experiment will use a comparative research study and a three by two factorial design to prove that there will be a statistically significant difference between students attending traditional and online modes of education, while at the same time comparing their academic performance in three subject categories of theoretical, technical, and mathematical.

The null hypothesis on the other hand, states that this experiment will use a three by two factorial design to prove that there will be no statistically significant difference between students attending traditional and online modes of education while at the same time comparing their academic performance in three subject categories of theoretical, technical, and mathematical.

Theoretical Framework

The program is forecasted to be delivered to two classes simultaneously, traditional, and online. The two courses will follow the same school calendar and will start and end at the same time to ensure examinations are equitable. The program must ensure all prerequisites are met and entry requirements are the same for both classes. It is also important to note the educational and work experience of the students. The curriculum and course material should be identical for both classes and are delivered by the same group of professors. The examinations for both groups should be the same while all students should be required to take them at the same time. These factors are important to provide a balanced and fair evaluation of both groups to produce effective comparative results. The major factors in this experiment include several subjects that include theoretical studies, technical activities that require hands-on work and experimentation that include mathematical formulas and calculations. This experiment will attempt to prove if there is a statistically significant difference in academic performance of students attending traditional classes and comparing them to online students, while including the variables of several subject categories.

Research Design

This study will focus on using a comparative research method and a simple factorial research design to evaluate postgraduate university students attending traditional modes and online modes of education. The primary data source for this project is based on research gathered from students attending several courses in information systems technologies.

The program is geared to provide students with new generation of technical knowledge to better prepare them to meet the demands of the marketplace. This experiment involves a three by two factorial design: grouping subjects in three categories of theoretical, technical, and mathematical. The other two levels are traditional and online modes of education. The following graph depicts the different combinations:

Traditional Mode
Online Mode
Theoretical
Technical
Mathematical

The first three factors in this experiment introduces basic concepts in theoretical subjects, while the technical subjects offer hands on activities and the mathematical courses offer formulas and calculations. This experiment will determine if there is statistically significant difference in academic performance of students in three subject categories while attending traditional and online modes of education. This comparative and simple factorial experiment will attempt to compute and analyze descriptive statistics for the groups represented in the different combinations of traditional and online students.

The mean scores will have to be computed for all six groups represented on the table above. The following steps will be required in analyzing the results of this factorial experiment by accomplishing an analysis of variance (ANOVA), analysis of covariance (ANCOVA) or a multiple regression analysis to determine whether the differences in mean scores are statistically significant.

Population and Sampling Design

A total of over 2000 graduate level students will be required to complete final examinations in order to compare the differences in scores in the three factors consisting of courses that measure subject categories of theoretical, technical, and mathematical and then investigating the differences between the two factors of delivery modes of education, both traditional and online.

The combination of the three by two factors produces a total of six different combinations in which comparisons can be made between traditional and online students. The main idea is to evaluate complete academic performance records of the two groups, keeping in mind that a larger population pool will give a better representation and accuracy in evaluating the performance between traditional and online students. Different statistical data analysis methods can be used to compare the two groups. For example, the t-test can be used to analyze differences in grades between traditional and online students. The independent t-test for example is most useful for determining if there is a difference in the mean scores of the two groups in question. Also, mean scores can be used to demonstrate which group received higher overall grade point averages.

A paired sample t-test is useful for describing the relationship between two variables, while statistically controlling for another variable. A partial correlation assists you in examining the strength and direction of the linear relationship between two variables, while controlling for another variable. Two-way Analysis of Variance (ANOVA) is the two-way between groups ANOVA which involves the simultaneous examination of two independent variables and one dependent variable.

Data Collection

Data collection consists of observational data, interview information, questionnaire data, and standardized test scores.

In this study all four methods data collection methods can be used to provide not only quantitative but qualitative results. These different approaches of data collection and measurements can ensure the research is assessing all the different relationships that can exist.

To perform a comparison between the two groups, a t-test can be used to demonstrate the differences between traditional and online students' academic performance. In addition, the mean scores of both groups can be used as a measure of whether traditional students performed better, the same, or worse than online students.

Data analysis is a computational process of descriptive statistics that measures group mean and standard deviation. The data tested for statistical significance includes variance, median, rank scores and frequencies. The t-test can be used for measuring the significant difference between mean scores in the two samples. Analysis of Variance (ANOVA) is used when more than two groups are studied.

The t-test for multiple comparisons is used to test the significance of the differences between two population means and it is completed after ANOVA to show significant difference between group scores and individual scores. Nonparametric test includes statistical significance that does not rely on any assumptions about the shape or variance of the population scores that include Chi-square, Mann-Whitney Test, and Wilcoxon Signed Rank Test.

Core Terms

According to Gall (2010) statistics is described as a set of procedures and rules for reducing large amounts of data to manageable sizes that can easily use to allow conclusions based on the data represented. Statistics also requires the use of arithmetic or algebraic algorithms with the capability to manipulation and apply data. Descriptive statistics on the other hand is used to simply describe a set of data that is used for a experiment. Statistical population is concerned with statistical inferences based on random sampling which are taken from population entities.

Inferential statistics is a process of drawing conclusions from data that are dependent to variation and are used as measures of a population (Gall, 2010). Samples require less effort and are derived from a population to predict the outcome of the whole. Statistics are considered numerical values that assist in summarizing the sampled data while parameters are numerical values that help in summarizing population data (Gall, 2010). Random sample is important in statistics and it helps in providing the best possible selection of a population under study, as a sample in which each member of the population has an equal chance of being included in the experiment or study.

The distinction between descriptive and inferential statistics is that descriptive statistics deal with simply describing a set of data by computing measures such as the average of the scores in our sample or how widely scores are distributed around that average (Gall, 2010). Inferential statistics, on the other hand, deal with making an inference from the data at hand to the overall population of objects from which the sample came.

When researchers must measure a population, it is usually based on sampling and many consider this to be the driving force behind statistics (Gall, 2010). When scientists study entire populations this is referred as a parameter. The other important concept to consider is the distinction between measurement data (measurement) and categorical data (Gall, 2010).

The idea of measurement consists of different levels or scales of measurement with nominal scales representing name of things, ordinal scales place items in increasing or decreasing order, interval scales specify the differences between points on a scale, and finally ratio scales are represented by comparative figures (Gall, 2010). There are also several different types of variables; continuous variables are any value between the lowest and highest points, whereas discrete variables include limited number of values with nothing in between (Gall, 2010). Also, dependent variables are the variables that we measure, whereas independent variables are depended on the researcher and their study (Gall, 2010). Random sampling determines the selection process of selecting the object for measuring and random assignment refers to the methods of assigning subject to different groups (Gall, 2010). Continuous variable provides an array of possible data while discrete variables consist of a determined set of values to me measured. Dependent variables are variables that are measured during the study and independent variable provide the flexibility to manipulate the data.

Symmetric distribution is a distribution that has the same shape on either side of the center and trimmed sample is a sample with a fixed percentage of scores deleted from each end (Gall, 2010). The normal distribution is a very common distribution in statistics, and it is often taken as a good description of how observations on a dependent variable are distributed. The normal distribution is a symmetric distribution with its mode at the center.

In fact, the mode, median, and mean will be the same for a variable that is normally distributed. We can convert raw scores on a normal distribution to z scores by simply dividing the deviation of the raw score from the population mean by the standard deviation of the population. The z score is an important statistic because it allows us to use tables of the standard's normal distribution. Once we convert a raw score to a z score, we can immediately use the tables of the standard normal distribution to compute the probability that any observation will fall within a given interval.

Measures of central tendency are numerical values that refer to the center of the distribution. The three common measures of central tendency are the mode, the median, and the mean. The mode can be defined simply as the most common score, the score obtained from the largest number of subjects (Gall, 2010). The median is most easily defined as the middle score in an ordered set or data. The most common measure of central tendency is the mean, or simply described as the average (Gall, 2010).

The mean is the sum of the scores divided by the number of scores. Histogram is graph in which a rectangle is used to represent frequencies of observations within each interval. Symmetric is having the same shape on both sides of the center. Bimodal: A distribution having two distinct peaks. Uni-modal is a distribution having one distinct peak. Modality is the number of meaningful peaks in a frequency distribution of the data.

Negatively skewed is a distribution that trails off to the left. Positively skewed is a distribution that trails off to the right. A z score represents the number of standard deviations that is above or below the mean while a positive z score being above the mean and a negative z score being below the mean (Gall, 2010). The probability calculated from the z is an approximation which is valid only for large values of n and is therefore most significant for experiments with many individual populations (Gall, 2010).

Bivariate correlation is useful for describing the relationship between two variables it describes both the strength and direction between the two variables (Szapkiw, 2010). Begin a bivariate correlation by generating a scatter plot to check for assumptions of homoscedasticity and assumptions of linearity. The first step in examining a scatter diagram is to check for outliers, outliers are essentially data points that are far away from the cluster.

The second step is to check for violations of assumptions (homoscedasticity and linearity). If the cluster is a cigar shape, this indicates that the assumptions of homoscedasticity are tenable. Also, if you can draw a straight line through the main cluster to check for tenability and to indicate either a positive or negative correlation. The third step determines the strength and direction of the relationship, an upward trend indicates a positive relationship and a downward trend indicates a negative relationship. The bivariate correlation plays a critical role in examining the strength and direction of the linear relationship between two population variables (Szapkiw, 2010).

A partial correlation assists you in examining the strength and direction of the linear relationship between two variables, while controlling for another variable (Szapkiw, 2010). A paired sample t-test is useful for describing the relationship between two variables, while statistically controlling for another variable (Szapkiw, 2010). Bivariate linear regression is useful for examining the ability of the independent or predictor variable to predict the dependent of criterion variable (Szapkiw, 2010). Bivariate linear regression uses two variables, continuous or one independent continuous variable and one dichotomous dependent variable (Szapkiw, 2010).

Linearity assumes that the relationship between the two variables is linear (Szapkiw, 2010). Check for linearity using a scatter plot; a roughly straight line indicates that the assumption is tenable (Szapkiw, 2010). Homoscedasticity assumes the variability in scores in both variables should be similar (Szapkiw, 2010). Check for homoscedasticity using a scatter plot; a cigar shape indicates that the assumption is tenable (Szapkiw, 2010).

One-way Analysis of Variance (ANOVA) is the one-way between groups ANOVA that involves the examination of an independent variable with three or more levels or groups and one dependent variable (Szapkiw, 2010). This demonstrates when there is a difference in the mean scores of the dependent variable across three or more groups. If statistical significance is found, post hoc tests need to be run to determine between which groups differences lie (Szapkiw, 2010). Two-way Analysis of Variance (ANOVA) is the two-way between groups ANOVA which involves the simultaneous examination of two independent variables and one dependent variable (Szapkiw, 2010). This procedure allows you to test for an interaction effect as well as the main effect of each independent variable (Szapkiw, 2010). If a significant interaction effect is found, additional analysis will be needed.

The One-way Repeated Measures Analysis of Variance (ANOVA) is the one-way repeated measures ANOVA which is used when you want to measure subjects of the same dependent variable three or more times (Szapkiw, 2010). It is also used to measure subjects' that are exposed to three different conditions or to measure subjects' responses to two or more different questions on a scale (Szapkiw, 2010). This procedure informs you if differences exist within a group among three sets of scores.

In Type I Errors the researcher rejects the null hypothesis when the null hypothesis is true, the researcher makes a Type

I error (Szapkiw, 2010). In Type II Errors the researcher fails to reject the null hypothesis when the null hypothesis is false, the researcher makes a Type II error (Szapkiw, 2010). Power can be influenced by the sample size, effect size, and alpha level; based on this information, increasing sample size is one of the most obvious ways to reduce both types of errors (Szapkiw, 2010). Paired sample t tests (also known as the repeated measures t tests) are used when you want to compare the mean scores of one groups at two different times (Szapkiw, 2010). Pretest/posttests are an example of the type of situation in which you may choose to use this procedure (Szapkiw, 2010). You may also use this procedure when you want to examine the same person in terms of his or her response to two questions (Szapkiw, 2010).

Significance of the Proposed Study

This case study provided the opportunity to investigate the impact of online education on society while choosing the appropriate statistical methods to satisfy the question proposed in this study. The variables used in this experiment consisted of independent variables of traditional and online education and the dependent variable of students' grade point averages. The results of the statistical tests are significant in indicating differences between the scores of students in traditional classes with their counterparts of online students. It is important to get a total number of students under the study along with using an equal grading scale. The statistical mean scores between the traditional and online students will need to be compared for any deviation between the groups.

The results will signify if there are differences in performance between traditional and online students. Finally, it is important to see if the research failed to reject the null hypotheses of disproving that there is no statistically significant difference between the performance of traditional and online students.

Core Research Assumptions

Most experiments have a certain number of variables that are extremely difficult to measure, while in this experiment the conditions have been set to provide the most accurate results possible under the constraints of access to data and facilities. Teaching styles and delivery methods can be considered manipulated factors and the researcher must be aware of these intrinsic conditions. The different exam scores of the individuals in the groups can be potential manipulated because of outside knowledge or expertise that the students bring into the program. The family socioeconomic environmental factors are more fixed and are not under the control of the experimenter. Also, physical characteristics cannot be under control of the experimenter such as age, gender, height, weight, or race. Through greater emphases and awareness of the unintended outcomes, school educators and policy makers can work to minimize the negative effects of testing on students.

The key is to maintain the testing environment for both the experimental and control groups as identical as possible. If variables outside the parameters of the experiment are introduced to the pretest and posttest conditions at any time of the process it may skew the test score results.

For example, if students are aware, they are going to be given a pretest they may prepare more and effect the testing score results between the experimental and control group. The major threat to the internal validity of any control group experiment is the pre-existing differences rather than the treatment effect of the experiment (Gall, 2010). For this condition, the analysis of covariance is used to address this issue (Gall, 2010). The analysis of covariance statistically assists by reducing the initial effects of the group differences by compensating to the posttest means of both groups (Gall, 2010).

References

A comparative study of student performance in traditional mode and online mode of learning.

Computer Applications in Engineering Education, 15(1), 30-40. doi:10.1002/cae.20092

Amanda Szapkiw, (2010), Statistics Guide, Liberty University

Gall, D. G., Gall. J. P., and Borh, W. R. (2010) Educational Research: An Introduction. Pearson

Qiping, S., Chung, J. H., Challis, D., & Cheung, R. T. (2007

Methodology

In a quantitative research project, it is typical of educational researchers first to identify their topic and ask specific questions to narrow their research topic. Researchers also collect data and analyze their findings by using statistics tools to ensure unbiased research. The development of quantitative research requires the use of statistical procedures that use several different measurement techniques. This research study will integrate the use of a comparative experiment to evaluate the differences between learning performance of traditional modes of education with technology driven online distance education.

This research study will be using a comparative and simple factorial research designs to evaluate university students attending traditional classes and online courses. This research study will investigate if there is a difference in academic performance between traditional modes of education and online delivery modes of education by evaluating final examination scores.

A population of over a few thousand university level students, spanning several years will be used for data gathering and comparative analysis purposes. This research will attempt to produce a comparison of the examination results between different delivery modes of study each year as well as between different classes over several years. Although it is believed that traditional mode students should be able to outperform their counterparts by scoring higher on final examinations and overall better performance records.

This research will attempt to answer many of the questions concerning the perceived differences between traditional and online students.

Proposed Research Design

Quantitative statistical research methods include the use of correlational procedures that compare different groups with resulting cause and effect relationships (Creswell, 2004). Quantitative testing and measurement techniques can be used to examine numerical data to predict achievement and performance (Creswell, 2004).

Quantitative educational research designs also involve the use of several different measurement techniques to include surveys and simple experimental methods to gauge the achievements of populations under study. The purpose of a research design addresses the need of the study and identifies the major issues concerning the research topic.

It is important for the researcher to identify the research process at the start of the research and most importantly identifying ethical considerations in conducting the research (Creswell, 2004). A good researcher constantly asks questions and will attempt to answer them using many different statistical and data analysis tools. Researchers provide a great service for society by addressing gaps in educational systems and improving processes while expanding the potential for knowledge on educational issues (Creswell, 2004).

Research provides the bases for educators to investigate and gain new ideas with further insight into processes and methods used in academic settings. Researchers also help stir up debate concerning existing policies and providing channels for recommending change and to assist in looking at different perspectives on issues of concern. Researchers provide the greatest value to students by helping them build sound research skills that include organizational, analytical, writing, and presentation skills (Creswell, 2004). Some of the problems with many research projects are the vagueness and contradictory findings that include questionable data with unclear results (Creswell, 2004).

The last few decades have produced dramatic technological advances in information technologies and other scientific fields that were never imagined possible not long ago. These technological advances have facilitated many industries to work and do things smarter. One sector that has been able to use these technological innovations is the educational community with initiatives such as online programs made possible by the internet and delivered through the web-based applications. With the rapid additions of online educational programs individuals are finding that furthering their education has never been easier.

The purpose of this research study is to compare student performance between traditional learning environments and distance learning modes. The population under study will be required to complete final examinations that will be used in comparing differences in examination scores in the three factors consisting of courses that measure subject categories of theoretical, technical, and mathematical and then investigating the differences between the two factors of delivery modes of education, both traditional and online. The primary data source for this project will be based on research gathered from students attending several courses in information systems technologies.

The traditional and online university programs in this study are geared towards providing students with many options to further their education eliminating any obstacles of time and distance. The goals of these programs are aimed at delivering access to education by various forms of online media available on demand. This research study uses a comparative research study and a simple factorial research design evaluating university students attending traditional modes and online modes of education.

This experiment will use a three by two factorial design: grouping subjects in three categories of theoretical, technical, and mathematical. The two levels within the design compare the differences between traditional and online modes of education. The first three factors in this experiment introduce basic concepts in theoretical subjects, and the technical subjects' category offer hands on activities and the mathematical courses offer formulas and calculations. This experiment will determine if there is statistically significant difference in academic performance of students in three subject categories while attending traditional and online modes of education.

The hypothesis of this experiment states, that this experiment will use a three by two factorial design to prove that there will be a statistically significant difference between students attending traditional and online modes of education while comparing their academic performance in three subject categories of theoretical, technical, and mathematical. The null hypothesis of this experiment will use a three by two factorial design to prove that there will be no statistically significant difference between students attending traditional and online modes of education while comparing their academic performance in three subject categories of theoretical, technical, and mathematical.

Logical Rationale of Research Method

The research cycle requires a complete systematic approach that includes identification, review, purpose, data collection, analysis and interpretation, and evaluation and reporting (Creswell, 2004). The research cycle is a continuous process that is always evolving and is need of constant retooling and scrutiny. A researcher first identifies a research problem and providing justification for need of the study (Creswell, 2004). Researchers will review many sources that are not limited to libraries, books, professional journals, electronic resources, and others (Creswell, 2004).

In selecting resources, a researcher determines the relevance of each resource and organizing them categorically for ease of access. It is also important for a researcher to narrow the research purpose statements to the topic at hand. In the data collection process, a researcher identifies his population, obtains permission, and gathers data (Creswell, 2004). In analyzing and interpreting data researchers attempt to break down the information into more manageable forms and be able to explain the findings to a review board if required (Creswell, 2004).

In reporting and evaluating of the finding's researchers structure the organization of the documentations and ensuring the accuracy of the final report while taking into consideration the audience (Creswell, 2004). Considering today's creditability concerns ethical considerations should be a top priority for a researcher, honoring the rights of the participants is paramount. The skills needed for research require individuals that have a natural curiosity to investigate and the ability to use technology for their benefit.

Educational research is the systematic collection and analysis of empirical data in order to develop valid, generalized knowledge that involves descriptions of educational phenomena, predictions about future events or performance, evidence about the effects of experimental interventions, and explanations of observed phenomena in terms of the basic processes (Gall, 2010). Quantitative research design internal validity, extent to which extraneous variables are controlled, so that observed effects can be attributed solely to the independent variable.

To derive research results for this study several different types of statistical data analysis were conducted. The data was first screened for outliers, distributional properties, and parametric assumptions. Diagnostic accuracy is addressed by way of a conditional probability analysis that requires a starting diagnostic point in making prediction outcomes (Gall, 2010).

Proportion outcome are a result of diagnostic accuracy analysis based on sensitivity, specificity, positive predictive power, and negative predictive power (Gall, 2010). Sensitivity and specificity provide a way to measure the accuracy of the predictor to identify the presence or absence of a given condition (Gall, 2010). Positive and negative predictive powers on the other hand measure efficiency by predicting correctly between who will be identified or not by the criterion measure, once a diagnostic status is known (Gall, 2010).

Educational researchers have been interested in offering alternative ways of education to reach the masses. For the last two decades educational institutions have increased online courses and programs to fill the needs of individuals and the marketplace. This case study provided the opportunity to investigate the impact of online education on society while choosing the appropriate statistical methods to satisfy the question proposed in this study.

The variables used in this experiment consisted of independent variables of traditional and online education and the dependent variable of students' grade point averages. The results of the statistical tests are significant in indicating differences between the scores of students in traditional classes with their counterparts of online students. It is important to get a total number of students under the study along with using an equal grading scale.

The statistical mean scores between the traditional and online students will need to be compared for any deviation between the groups. The results will signify if there are differences in performance between traditional and online students. Finally, it is important to see if the research failed to reject the null hypotheses of disproving that there is no statistically significant difference between the performance of traditional and online students.

Units of Analysis

In collecting quantitative data, a researcher needs to ask, who will be under study and the type of sampling size or unit will be required (Gall, 2010). Also, researchers need to investigate what level of permissions will be required before venturing in depth into their research. In addition, it is important to identify what information will be required to collect and what type of data available. The selections of statistical instruments are required in identifying the scales of measurement and validity and reliability of the data (Gall, 2010). Unit of analysis is the level at which the data will be gathered (Gall, 2010).

There may be different units of analysis, one for the dependent variable and another for one for the independent variable.

This research study focuses on educational program that is forecasted to be delivered to two classes simultaneously, traditional, and online. The two courses will follow the same school calendar and will start and end at the same time to ensure examinations are equitable. The educational program must ensure both modes of education meet all prerequisites and entry requirements are the same for both set of students. It is also important to note the educational and work experience of the students.

The curriculum and course material should be identical for both classes and are delivered by the same group of professors. The examinations for both groups should be the same while all students should be required to take them at the same time. These factors are important to provide a balanced and fair evaluation of both groups to produce effective comparative results.

Over several thousand graduate level students will be required to complete final examinations to get a large enough population for this study and to compare further details of examination of test scores. Three categories of theoretical, technical, and mathematical will be used measure the differences between traditional and online students' scores in their respected subjects.

Points of Focus

With the rapid advances in technology, educational institutions have adopted to offer alternative modes of education to meet student needs. This study will be based on the statistical results of college students attending traditional and online courses over several different courses while comparing final examination scores between both groups. The goal of this study is to compare traditional modes of education with online modes of education and determine if there is statistically significant difference in academic performance by evaluating final student examination scores.

This study will focus on a population sample size of over a few thousand students observed over a span of several years attending traditional and online modes of education settings, in order to gather the largest sampling required to produce the most statistically accurate results. This research requires the data collection consisting and comparing academic examination scores of students in similar courses while evaluating the impact of the modes of delivery. In order to determine the sampling, it is important to choose students with the same experience along with consistent teachers with similar experience and background.

There are a multitude of samplings that can determine the selection of students for this research and that includes age, race, learning style, socio-economic status, and environmental conditions. To draw comparisons between both homogeneous groups of traditional and online student's, quantitative analysis of student performance should be based on final examination scores. When comparing homogeneous groups, it is important to control for extraneous variables with respect to the extraneous variables and limitations.

Dependent and Independent Variables

Educators and students have been interested in decades in comparing the performance of students in technology driven distance learning courses and attending live lectures on campus. With the convenience of attending online classes many wonder if they are getting their monies worth in receiving a quality education. Another concern with online education is the lack of interaction between students and teachers as compared to live face-to-face lecture traditional schools offer. This case study provided the opportunity to investigate the impact of online education on society while choosing the appropriate statistical methods to satisfy the question proposed in this study.

The variables used in this experiment consisted of independent variables of traditional and online education and the dependent variable of students' grade point averages. The results of the statistical tests are significant in indicating differences between the scores of students in traditional classes with their counterparts of online students. It is important to get a total number of students under the study along with using an equal grading scale.

The statistical mean scores between the traditional and online students will need to be compared for any deviation between the groups. The results will signify if there are differences in performance between traditional and online students. Finally, it is important to see if the research failed to reject the null hypotheses of disproving that there is no statistically significant difference between the performance of traditional and online students.

It is important to realize that this study will be faced with many variables, for example difficulty of course subjects and materials. The type of delivery method can also have the potential to influence the performance of the students as compared to traditional and online students. To deliver students with the same experience it is important to consider teachers experience along with identifying the background of the students.

There are a multitude of variables that can determine the performance of students; student age, race, learning style, socio- economic status, and environmental conditions such as time of day, location, and temperature. To draw comparisons of traditional education to online modes of instruction, quantitative analysis of student performance based on numerical examination scores must be used.

The research study will take into consideration the following variables and conditions: Delivery of traditional and online classes on the same schedule, with the same start and end dates. Provide the same prerequisites along with equal entry requirements. Ensure course design and learning material is the same and equally accessible and delivered by the same teachers. Provide the same examination to both groups and evaluate using the same grading scale. These factors should provide a stable and appropriate comparison for conducting this study in determining the learning effectiveness of traditional and online educational modes.

Measurement of Variables

Measurement instruments are tools that are used in observation or documentation of quantitative data (Gall, 2010). There are several types of instruments for example performance measures are used to test performance, attitudinal measure attitudes and feelings toward education policies, behavioral measures are used for observation purposes, factual measures record data, and linking the data to experimental variables (Gall, 2010). A factorial experiment for instance determines the effect of two or more independent variables, both individually and in combination with each other as compared to a dependent variable (Gall, 2010).

The main effect measures the impact of the independent variable on the dependent variable (Gall, 2010). This interaction between the independent and dependent variables is called an interaction effect. In research studies requiring two-by two designs four treatment groups are established with each group receiving different combinations of the two main factors (Gall, 2010). In factorial research designs participants should be randomly assigned to the four treatment groups. A research experiment involving a three-by-two factorial design has six combinations of factors; it normally would require six groups of students (Gall, 2010).

In a control group design, it is required to maintain the experimental and control groups as identical as possible (Gall, 2010). If variables outside the parameters of the experiment are introduced to the pretest and posttest conditions at any time of the process it may skew the test score results. For example, if students are aware, they are going to be given a pretest they may prepare more and effect the testing score results between the experimental and control group.

The major threat to the internal validity of a nonequivalent control group experiment is the pre- existing differences rather than the treatment effect of the experiment (Gall, 2010). For this condition, the analysis of covariance is used to address this issue (Gall, 2010). The analysis of covariance statistically assists by reducing the initial effects of the group differences by compensating to the posttest means of both groups (Gall, 2010).

Nature of the Population

A group of individuals with similar characteristics make up a population and a sub-group is considered a sample of the target population (Gall, 2010). Researchers use target populations for the purpose of making predictions and generalizations (Gall, 2010). Population samplings are used as estimates for comparing differences between the sample estimate and the true population and this is labeled as sampling error (Gall, 2010). On the other hand, probability sampling is when individuals are representatives of a population under study.

Also, non-probability sampling consists of individuals that are selected to participate in a study because of their availability or possess special characteristics (Gall, 2010). There are also several other types of probability samples that include simple random samples which have equal chance of being selected for the study (Gall, 2010). Systematic sampling requires selecting individuals based on a certain predetermined set of numbers. The multi-stage cluster sampling includes individuals selected in different stages or times (Gall, 2010). Stratified sampling requires identifying individuals based on characteristic such as gender (Gall, 2010). Non-probability samples include convenience sampling of individuals being selected because they are willing and available (Gall, 2010). In snowball sampling, researchers involve individuals to identify other participants to become members of the sample population.

The students in this research study will be required to complete final examinations in order to compare the differences in scores in the three factors consisting of courses that measure subject categories of theoretical, technical, and mathematical and then investigating the differences between the two factors of delivery modes of education, both traditional and online. The combination of the three by two factors produces a total of six different combinations in which comparisons can be made between traditional and online students.

The main idea is to evaluate complete academic performance records of the two groups, keeping in mind that a larger population pool will give a better representation and accuracy in evaluating the performance between traditional and online students. Different statistical data analysis methods can be used to compare the two groups. For example, the t-test can be used to analyze differences in grades between traditional and online students.

The independent t-test for example is most useful for determining if there is a difference in the mean scores of the two groups in question. Also, mean scores can be used to demonstrate which group received higher overall grade point averages. A paired sample t-test is useful for describing the relationship between two variables, while statistically controlling for another variable. A partial correlation assists you in examining the strength and direction of the linear relationship between two variables, while controlling for another variable. Two-way Analysis of Variance (ANOVA) is the two-way between groups ANOVA which involves the simultaneous examination of two independent variables and one dependent variable.

Typically, a larger population sample size increases the accuracy and precision in estimating various attributes of a population under experimentation. This study will measure the test results of several thousand students randomly chosen over a period of several semesters. It is important to consider the statistical rules of the law of large numbers and the central limit theorem, supporting the sampling distribution of the mean approaching normal distribution. The problem many researchers face is calculating the sample size required to reach normal distribution while considering extraneous factors and variables.

Data Collection Strategy

Procedures for administering the data collection process include: developing standard written procedures for administering of the data, collecting observational data, obtaining permission to collect and use public documents, and research ethics in respecting individuals and sites during data gathering (Creswell, 2004). Data collection consists of observational data, interview information, questionnaire data, and standardized test scores (Creswell, 2004). In this study all four methods data collection methods can be used to provide not only quantitative but qualitative results. These different approaches of data collection and measurements can ensure the research is assessing all the different relationships that can exist.

To perform a comparison between the two groups, a t-test can be used to demonstrate the differences between traditional and online students' academic performance. In addition, the mean scores of both groups can be used as a measure of whether traditional students performed better, the same, or worse than online students.

Data analysis is a computational process of descriptive statistics that measures group mean and standard deviation. The data tested for statistical significance includes variance, median, rank scores and frequencies. The t-test can be used for measuring the significant difference between mean scores in the two samples. Analysis of Variance (ANOVA) is used when more than two groups are studied.

The t-test for multiple comparisons is used to test the significance of the differences between two population means and it is completed after ANOVA to show significant difference between group scores and individual scores. Nonparametric test includes statistical significance that does not rely on any assumptions about the shape or variance of the population scores that include Chi-square, Mann-Whitney Test, and Wilcoxon Signed Rank Test.

In this research project the data collection method will consist of comparing academic performance records between the students in the same program of study to evaluate the impact of online learning. Student performance should be measured by their grade point averages in each subject matter in accordance with the university or college grading guidelines. To perform a comparison between the two groups, a t-test can be used to demonstrate the differences between traditional and online students' academic performance. In addition, the mean scores of both groups can be used to calculate the average academic grades. On a final note, it is important to have a large enough sample size to study and evaluate to provide the most accurate statistical results possible. The longitudinal cross-sectional studies may play a major role in comparing traditional students to online students regarding variables such as age, race, experience, and environmental conditions.

In analyzing data from a pretest and posttest control group experiment it is ideal to compute descriptive statistics. Descriptive statistics attempts to summarize the bulk of quantitative data while making inferences about population under investigation. The mean scores are required for the experimental and control groups to measure for statistical differences between the groups. To reduce systematic favoritism, random sampling selection of students may be incorporated during all stages of this study.

The ideal statistical method is analysis of covariance (ANCOVA), in which the posttest means of the experimental group is compared with the posttest mean of the control group with the pretest scores used as a covariate (Gall, 2010). If the assumptions underlying ANCOVA cannot be satisfied, it may better to consider an analysis of variance of the posttest means (Gall, 2010). Because there are two posttest means, one for the experimental group and one for the control group, this is equivalent to doing a t-test (Gall, 2010).

Another approach is to do a two-way analysis of variance for repeated measures (Gall, 2010). The quasi-experimental design most used in educational research is the nonequivalent control group design. In the nonequivalent control group design, research participants are not randomly assigned to the experimental and control groups while both groups are treated the same by taking a pretest and a posttest (Gall, 2010).

Institutional Review Board

The process for obtaining research permission includes institutional, site- specific, individual, campus approval, and Institutional Review Board (IRB). It is important to know the mission statement of the Institutional Review Board (IRB) at University and it states, "The University Institutional Review Board (IRB) exists to protect the rights and welfare of human participants volunteering in any academic research study. All human subjects' research at University must be approved by the IRB." The first step in the review process is to determine if an IRB review is needed in the first place.

In class assignments are managed by the instructor and most class assignments do not need IRB review. Students enrolled in master's theses and doctoral dissertations most likely will be required to apply for an IRB review. If portion of a student's research are used towards their dissertation a separate approval will be required. The second step in the IRB approval process students are required to secure a faculty sponsor.

The faculty sponsor will also be a student's chair during the IRB review. Also, students enrolled in a master's program working on their theses will be required to have a sponsor. For students requiring IRB during a class the instructor will serve as the sponsor. The role of the faculty sponsor is to facilitate your dissertation or theses while ensuring ethical standards are upheld. The third step of the IRB review requires the appropriate application and forms are used. If a student's research involves use of various media sources, they will be more likely required to complete a Research Exemption Request form. The projects that fall under this category will generally take up to one month to review. For research that does not require the Research Exemption Request criteria, students will be required to complete the Expedited/Full Review form. Research projects in this category will take up to two months for an IRB review. The IRB review process consists of three categories: exempt research, expedited review, and full committee review. The fourth step in the review process requires students to view the avoiding pitfalls section of the IRB homepage.

The fifth step in the review process serves as check list of a completed application. Keep in mind that the application requires student's signature along with the students sponsor for the application to be complete. The sixth step requires the submission of the correct IRB application forms.

Data Analysis Procedures

Data analysis is a computational process of descriptive statistics that measures population mean scores and standard deviation statistical differences (Gall, 2010). The data tested for measuring statistical significance includes variance, median, rank scores and frequencies. For example, the t-test can be used for measuring the significant difference between mean scores between two samples. Analysis of Variance (ANOVA) is used when more than two groups are studied.

The t-test for multiple comparisons is used to test the significance of the differences between two population means and is completed after ANOVA to demonstrate significant differences between group scores and individual scores. Nonparametric testing includes statistical significance that does not rely on any assumptions concerning the shape or variance of population scores, including Chi-square, Mann-Whitney Test, and Wilcoxon Signed Rank Test.

Statistics is described as a set of procedures and rules for reducing large amounts of data to manageable sizes that can easily use to allow conclusions based on the data represented. Statistics also requires the use of arithmetic or algebraic algorithms with the capability to manipulation and apply data (Gall, 2010). Descriptive statistics on the other hand is used to simply describe a set of data that is used for an experiment. Statistical population is concerned with statistical inferences based on random sampling which are taken from population entities (Gall, 2010).

Inferential statistics is a process of drawing conclusions from data that are dependent to variation and are used as measures of a population (Gall, 2010). Samples require less effort and are derived from a population to predict the outcome of the whole. Statistics are considered numerical values that assist in summarizing the sampled data while parameters are numerical values that help in summarizing population data (Gall, 2010). Random sample is important in statistics and it helps in providing the best possible selection of a population under study, as a sample in which each member of the population has an equal chance of being included in the experiment or study.

The distinction between descriptive and inferential statistics is that descriptive statistics deal with simply describing a set of data by computing measures such as the average of the scores in our sample or how widely scores are distributed around that average (Gall, 2010).

Inferential statistics, on the other hand, deal with making an inference from the data at hand to the overall population of objects from which the sample came. When researchers have to measure a population, it is usually based on sampling and many consider this to be the driving force behind statistics (Gall, 2010). When scientists study entire populations this is referred as a parameter. The other important concept to consider is the distinction between measurement data (measurement) and categorical data (Gall, 2010).

Descriptive statistics research study summarizes the collection of quantitative data while providing statistical inferences concerning the population involved in the experiment (Gall, 2010). The mean scores are required for the experimental and control groups to measure for statistical differences between the groups.

To reduce systematic favoritism, random sampling selection of students may be incorporated during all stages of this study. The control group design requires maintain the experimental and control groups as identical as possible (Gall, 2010). If variables outside the parameters of the experiment are introduced to the pretest and posttest conditions at any time of the process it may skew the test score results. For example, if students are aware, they are going to be given a pretest they may prepare more and effect the testing score results between the experimental and control group.

Analytical Approach

When researchers are involved in a casual comparative research study, they seek to identify cause and affect relationships. They do this by organizing separate groups to determine whether the individuals differ on a predetermined dependent experimental variable.

An important feature of a comparative research study is the fact that a comparative measurement is made between the independent and the dependent groups (Creswell, 2004).

Nominal or ordinal scales of measurement are used in interpretation of results of the data (Creswell, 2004). In addition, the independent variable is measured using interval or ratio scales. A correlation research design is most often used for analyzing data of independent and dependent variables. Also, most causal comparative research designs can be characterized as a type of correlation research design by simply altering how the variables are measured or analyzed.

Researchers often prefer to use a causal comparative design for two reasons, to measure independent variable and the ease of interpreting and comprehending the findings. A causal comparative research studies can vary to include one independent or dependent variable or several in a study. The researcher is offered flexibility in choosing the statistical analysis methods to meet the needs of the study involving the investigation of independent and dependent variables.

Statistical Procedures and Analytical Techniques

This research study uses both comparative and simple factorial experimental designs to compute and analyze descriptive statistics for the different groups represented in traditional and online classes. The mean scores are required for both categories, traditional and online students and to include the six subgroups represented in individual courses.

To accomplish a complete statistical analysis of this, experiment the ANOVA and ANCOVA or a multiple regression analysis will have to be accomplished in order to determine whether the differences in mean scores are statistically significant. In analyzing data for the pretest and posttest portion of this experiment it is ideal to compute descriptive statistics. The ideal statistical method is the ANCOVA, in which the posttest mean of the experimental group is compared with the posttest mean of the control group, with the pretest scores used as a covariate (Gall, 2010). If the assumptions underlying ANCOVA cannot be satisfied, it may better to consider an analysis of variance of the posttest means (Gall, 2010). Because there are two posttest means, one for the experimental group and one for the control group, this is equivalent to doing a t-test (Gall, 2010). Another approach is to do a two-way analysis of variance for repeated measures (Gall, 2010).

The quasi-experimental design most used in educational research is the nonequivalent control group design. In the nonequivalent control group design, research participants are not randomly assigned to the experimental and control groups while both groups are treated the same by taking a pretest and a posttest (Gall, 2010).

Proposed Research Schedule

An experimental research study is a major undertaking that requires a considerable time to finish and is generally accomplished in several different stages. The first thing a researcher must be concerned with is in identifying a significant research topic that will contribute significantly with new information or knowledge that could possibly use in improving processes (Gall, 2010). Researchers do need to consider available resources and expertise before starting their research study. The second stage involves in writing the research proposal and the process involved in accomplishing the research study (Gall, 2010).

The purpose statement of the research proposal describes the issues or problems that will be addressed in the study. The research process can include several procedures for data collection and analysis. Also, it is important you receive research approval from your university or dissertation board members prior approval before starting the data collection process. The third stage can include a pilot study to develop and attempt different methods of collecting data (Gall, 2010).

Also, many issues can be identified or solved before more intensive study can continue. This step can save a researcher much valuable time by identifying problems early in the research study. The fourth stage includes conducting the main research study collecting and analyzing the actual data that will be included in the final report of the dissertation (Gall, 2010).

The fifth stage requires preparation of the final dissertation report for doctoral students. Also, researchers could have their work reviewed by professional peers in journal articles or presentations. Depending on the research these stages can be altered or changed to fit the needs of the research project or the researcher.

References

Gall, D. G., Gall. J. P., and Borh, W. R. (2010) Educational Research: An Introduction, 8th Edition, Pearson

John W. Creswell (2004) Educational Research: Planning, Conducting, and Evaluating

Quantitative and Qualitative Research, 2nd Edition, Pearson

Liberty University (2011) Theses and Dissertations Publishing Guidelines, Retrieved from:

http://www.liberty.edu/index.cfm?PID=10522

Qiping, S., Chung, J. H., Challis, D., & Cheung, R. T. (2007). A comparative study of student performance in traditional mode and online mode of learning. Computer Applications in Engineering Education, 15(1), 30-40. doi:10.1002/cae.20092

High Stakes Testing and Student Motivation

The following research presentation examines high stakes testing policies as they relate to student motivation and learning. The main purpose of high-stakes testing initiatives and No Child Left Behind was to increase accountability as they relate to student achievement by mandating states to implement statewide assessments.

Political polices support high stakes testing with the idea of placing more accountability on educators while assuming that student motivation and learning would be increased. Several states have taken the lead by using high stakes testing to grant or withhold diplomas, leaving failing students with very few options. High- stakes testing may be having the opposite effect and, in many instances, has shown to decrease student motivation to learn.

Research trends have identified the most common reason students leave school early is due to the stresses associated with high stakes testing along with family issues. Research studies are leaning towards high stakes testing being more of detriment towards student staying in school, with less privileged social groups being hit the hardest. Even in today's political climate, high stakes testing initiatives are being hotly debated as other alternative strategies for improving student motivation and learning are investigated.

The main purpose of is presentation is investigating high stakes testing as it relates to student motivation and learning. The aim of the current federal government policies concerning high-stakes testing is to hold educators accountable by using student test results as a gauge to measure teaching and curriculum effectiveness. The high-stakes debate continues with many questioning the effectives of the program and whether its promise to increase accountability and student learning has been achieved. High-stakes initiatives continue to be popular amongst many political and educational leaders as a mechanism for holding educators accountable. High-stakes testing policies have triggered much debate to further examine whether its promise to increase student learning has been fulfilled. Some studies suggest that it may have the opposite effect on many students, especially in critical subject areas such as math, science, and writing.

Researchers support the idea that individuals are less likely to be intrinsically motivated to learn when subjected to the stresses associated with high-stakes testing. Additionally, teachers seem to take greater control of the learning environment, while denying the students opportunities to be responsible for their own learning. Future research is required to address the underlying issues stresses associated with high stakes testing as it relates to student motivation and learning.

How does increased high stakes standardized testing relate to student motivation?

Research Topic: This study examines the relationship between high stakes testing and student motivation to learn and excel in school.

Null Hypothesis: There is no relationship between high stakes testing given to students and students' motivation.

Non-directional Hypothesis: There is a relationship between the high stakes standardized tests given to students and students' motivation and attitude to learn.

Directional Hypothesis: As the number of high stakes standardized tests given to student's increases, their motivation decreases.

Educational research is the systematic collection and analysis of empirical data to develop valid, generalized knowledge that involves:

Descriptions of educational phenomena

Predictions about future events or performance

Evidence about the effects of experimental interventions

Explanations of observed phenomena in terms of the basic processes

The purpose of this study

What previous research is your study most directly based on?

How does your study build on previous research?

How will your study contribute to educational research and practice?

Research Questions, Hypotheses, Variables, and Case Delineation

Research questions or hypotheses.

Quantitative independent variable, a dependent variable, or neither

Qualitative data collection and analysis

Descriptive, causal, comparative, correlation, experimental, case study or specific qualitative research tradition, evaluative, or action research

Quantitative research design internal validity, extent to which extraneous variables are controlled, so that observed effects can be attributed solely to the independent variable.

Qualitative criteria to judging the credibility and trustworthiness of the results that will be yielded by your research design.

Sampling quantitative describe the characteristics of the population that you will study.

Qualitative describe the phenomenon you wish to study and the cases that comprise instances of the phenomenon.

Sampling procedure and sampling unit.

Size of your sample and explain why that sample size is sufficient.

Sample will be formed into subgroups, and characteristics of the subgroups.

Use of volunteers and their characteristics affecting the research findings.

Methods of Data Collection

Variables to study will be measured by a test, questionnaire, interview, observational procedure, or content analysis.

Investigate measures that are already available or whether they will need to be developed.

Types of validity and reliability are relevant and how you will check them.

Data-Analysis Procedures

Descriptive statistics and inferential statistics

Qualitative measures will use an interpretational, structural, or reflective method of analysis.

Ethics and Human Relations

Risks associated with study

Approved by an institutional review board.

Proposed research setting and gain the cooperation of your research participants.

A major obstacle to student motivation and learning may in fact be with the current grading system of raking and stacking individuals along with the stresses and anxieties related to high-stakes testing.

The grading system is creating an environment of competition that rewards the individual and does not promote teamwork.

Many professions rely on teamwork as an example in the military environment if the team fails the mission fails.

Team work and sharing of information with one another not only provides you with a positive feeling of knowing that you helped someone, it also creates a positive environment of sharing and trust that can be used to accomplish the task or mission in an more effective and efficient manner.

Researchers require the option to use multiple research methods to conduct studies that will address their research questions. No single method is well suited to answer complex research questions requiring in-depth study of multifaceted research topics. Individuals have feelings that are difficult to measure; they consist of intrinsic thoughts that are developed over time and experience.

Institutions on the other hand are process driven by data and statistical methods requiring various measurement techniques in assisting management to identify trends or problem areas. Mixed-method research uses both qualitative and quantitative techniques either concurrently or individually to address research questions. Mixed-method research provides many options for researchers to mix and match depending on whether they use qualitative methods to explain quantitative findings or the other way around.

The benefit of using mixed-method studies is that it does not impose any restrictions on type of measures to be used during the findings. In mixed- method research projects quantitative results are used for statistical analysis and qualitative results are used in observational settings.

The needs for multiple forms of research methods are important for experimentation to provide researchers with different perspectives and ideas during their findings.

Traditionally research methods have consisted of two camps, quantitative and qualitative.

Although researchers have debated on which method is superior the consensus remains that both quantitative and qualitative research methods complement each other. Researchers are more aware of the benefits of mixing both methods to address the same research topic.

It is important for researchers to have expertise in both quantitative and qualitative research methods to be able to provide well rounded studies.

Many researchers suggest breaking up research studies in phases of either quantitative or qualitative, with the 1st phase introducing the topic and the 2nd phase to support and to better understand the original findings.

In many instances' researchers are required to use formal research methods, but in their day-to-day activates many prefer action research to carry out their studies.

The main goal of action research is for researchers to use it in improving their processes within their profession.

Action research consists of many different variations that consist of teacher research, insider research, and self-study research, while offering then an opportunity to collaborate with other researchers.

The benefit of action research is that it is more practical for educators to use and carry out in everyday situations and to solve problems in real-time.

Action research is mostly used by professionals within their internal processes, but outsiders are used to evaluate or make recommendations on improving processes or interpret the findings.

Evaluation is another process that can be used by educators and researchers alike to measure the quality and effectiveness of research studies.

Evaluation studies help researchers to learn more about programs and to discover their effectives or need for implementation.

The major obstacle in conducting evaluations is that most research programs are different and require custom made forms of quality control measurements.

The evaluation model offers researchers opportunity to identify discrepancies within systems or processes while offering improvement initiatives and ideas.

Amrein and Berliner (2003) conducted research in several states currently using high stakes testing to grant or withhold diplomas. Their research has uncovered that high-stakes testing is having the opposite effect and it has shown to decrease student motivation to learn. State graduation statistics from this research study have identified trends of students leaving school early due to the stresses associated with high-stakes testing (Amrein & Berliner, 2003).

With state and federal high-stakes testing requirements along with personnel pressures and high family expectations students may be simply overwhelmed causing dropout rates to increase. The major issue with high-stakes testing is that a single exam score can determine the future and success in society for an individual; many never recover from this dramatic experience.

Jones (2007) identified that over 90% of participants in one study reported that teachers should be accountable for their teaching. Surveys and other forms of data collection contain many different variables that can be easily manipulated to achieve intended outcomes. Although the importance of holding teachers accountable can be highly debatable, it is important evaluate the intended and unintended outcomes of high-stakes testing.

Some of the unintended outcomes of high-stakes testing include using student test scores as a means to hold educators accountable, effects on instruction, effects on student and teacher motivation, and the effects on students who are at risk of failing or dropping out (Jones, 2007).

The author suggests that through greater emphases and awareness of the unintended outcomes of high-stakes testing, educators and policy makers can work to minimize the negative effects of standardized testing. Research has proven several unintended outcomes of high-stakes testing have been positive, many of the unintended outcomes have been negative. Although policy makers may be aware of the unintended outcomes associated with high-stakes testing, the question is what they can do about it, considering the political complexity and shear mass of the school system in America.

Booher-Jennings (2008) conducted a research project on several urban schools to study retention policies and how they relate to boys and girls failing high-stakes tests. Understanding how boys and girls experience high-stakes testing and whether they experience it differently was the focus of Booher-Jennings.

The authors discovered that teachers compared boys' failure to poor behavior and attitudes, while making the point that most girls needed more self-esteem to pass standardized exams. Recent media attention with the portrayal of females in more aggressive and heroin roles in movies may have contributed to a tightening of the gender gap between boys and girls while changing the perceived roles of females.

Sloan and Kelly (2003) investigated the alignment between high stakes testing and school curriculum, with the distinction between assessment of learning and assessment for testing. A major political driving force behind high-stakes testing initiatives in America has resulted because of the decline in student scores in math and science assessments compared to international students.

Policy makers have used these comparisons to support their agendas for the need of high stakes testing to hold teacher accountable and measure student performance. The result is that no test is valid or reliable while no test is above criticism (Sloan & Kelly, 2003). A major concern is that many individuals or groups criticize high stakes testing unfairly for their effects on student motivation for learning without sufficient data based on complexities of research.

According to Vogler and Virtue (2007) high-stakes testing has caused educators to teach using centered instructional practices, for example very formal traditional lectures with very little time for debate.

High-stakes testing has forced teachers to teach for the test, focusing on developing student's recall memory rather than allowing for creativity and other cognitive skills to flourish (Vogler & Virtue, 2007). Academic standards determine the growth and development of an individual, while also influencing student-teacher relationships.

Individuals at different stages of development have different needs and requirements; processes need to be in place to facilitate their learning and growth. Being aware of the stages of development teachers are better prepared to provide effective methods and strategies to better prepare and motivate their students.

Realizing that students have high energy and need to constantly be moving; developing curriculum around those needs, not only help the student feel at ease it also motivates them to learn and do better. High-stakes testing does not consider the importance of integrating hands on activities such as play acting and team building to help reinforce long term learning and personal growth.

According to Nichols (2007), high-stakes initiatives have held popularity amongst many political and educational leaders as a mechanism for holding educators accountable. High-stakes testing policies have triggered many research studies to examine whether it has fulfilled its promise to increase student motivation and teaching (Nichols, 2007). Nichols (2007) concludes that there is no consistent evidence to suggest high-stakes testing leads to increases in student motivation and learning. Some studies suggest that it may have the opposite effect on many students or groups in many critical subject areas.

Erick (2002) further investigated the use of hands on activities in the classroom and their effects on motivation and results on high-stakes testing scores. The author suggests that high-stakes testing has caused educators and students to focus more concentration on passing tests and memorizing questions rather than understanding and learning the material for the long term (Erick, 2002). High-stakes policies have placed additional pressures on educators by making student test scores public.

Many states have discovered through various interviews and surveys that high- stakes testing tends to place teachers under pressure to teach to the test (Nichols, 2007). Although there remains no consensus on the effects of high-stakes testing, studies do provide evidence that further research is needed to explore new and logical improvement initiatives. Another important study that needs further investigation is the introduction of no-stakes testing, with the intent of comparing the two systems to validate student efficiency and performance (Nichols, 2007).

The Florida Comprehensive Assessment Test (FCAT) is a high-stakes test that public school students must pass to be eligible for graduation from high school in Florida. Borg, Plumlee, and Stranahan, (2007) suggest that FCAT statistics prove that high-stakes tests results demonstrate differences on test scores depending on race and ethnicity. Their research finds that African American and Hispanic students coming from poorer, less educated households are less likely to meet graduation requirements than their higher socioeconomic white students.

African American students and students from the lowest income households are also the most likely to encounter a negative graduation effect because the passing score on the FCAT rises each year. The study also points out that school locations and characteristics affect the probability of student success on the FCAT. The study shows that high schools that hire more teachers with advanced degrees or offer a magnet program have better student FCAT scores. This results in higher probabilities that all categories of students will meet graduation requirements.

Meyer, McClure, Walkey, Weir, and McKenzie (2009) have identified several key characteristics such as competence motivation, achievement values, and goal orientations as they relate to standardized testing scores. The standards-based National Certificate of Educational Achievement (NCEA) was developed in New Zealand with the intention of strengthening connections between student learning behaviors and achievement outcomes. This study investigated interrelationships between self-reported motivation orientations and achievement outcomes on the NCEA, a standards-based, criterion-referenced assessment system for senior secondary students.

There were a total 3,569 of participants ages 11-3 from 20 nationally representative secondary schools in New Zealand. Survey data were factor analyzed followed by regression analyses to examine relationships across demographic factors, self-report survey results, and NCEA achievement outcomes. The results of several theoretically meaningful self-reported motivation orientations were strongly related to actual achievement including doing my best (high achievement) and doing just enough (low achievement). These dimensions varied by gender, ethnicity, and school zone. The author concluded that these findings illustrate how particular design features of a standards-based assessment system relate to student attitudes and achievement. They also highlight the need for longitudinal research to investigate patterns over time as well as the possible impact of interventions to alter motivation and/or academic task performance.

Berkowitz & Serim (2002) focused their research study using the significance of educational process improving initiatives effecting schools in America. They discuss several issues relating to student performance and motivation using information and new technology. Evidence suggests that annual testing has practically paralyzed any progress toward education reform and technology integration.

Fear-based responses initiated by high-stakes testing often sacrifice the higher thinking of special learning initiatives such as project-based learning approaches (Berkowitz & Serim, 2002). The problem with high-stakes testing is that it favors rote learning rather than using technology and creative thinking processes to dominate the school environment. The education system needs proven strategies that facilitate performance by improving thinking on the part of teachers and students alike.

Research design of high-stakes testing is based on the rational of threats and punishment as a mechanism to hold teachers accountable, while at the same time pressuring students to be more motivated (Nichols, 2007).

The theory of threats and punishment is based on authoritarian leadership techniques that have been proven to be effective in training new military recruits in basic training but offer very little incentive to more experienced and seasoned professional.

According to many policy makers, it is commonly held that high-stakes testing is effective because teachers are accountable thus in-turn will be further motivated to work harder and teach better (Nichols, 2007).

It is also assumed that students will work harder and learn more by being placed under pressure to perform well in their high-stakes tests; while high test scorers will feel good, poor test scorers will be forced to try and work harder. High-stakes tests provide an opportunity to measure student performance that can also be utilized by teachers to gauge their teaching effectiveness.

High-stakes testing was designed with the intent to place pressure on educators to teach to a set of objectives that can used to measure student performance (Nichols, 2007).

Rather, these high-stakes testing policies aimed at improving the educational system are working or not remains to be evidence is lacking for clear improvements in student learning.

Data collection and statistical analysis methods were used throughout the study comparing high stakes testing and students' motivation.

National Educational Longitudinal Survey (NELS) were used to report to prove that high-stakes testing had very little effect on student performance on math and reading achievement as reported in states with and without high-stakes tests (Nichols, 2007).

The NELS provided evidence that states with high-stakes tests had more dropouts than those without them (Nichols, 2007).

Comparing graduation rates and SAT scores in states with a graduation exam against states without a graduation exam, data identifies states with graduation exams had lower graduation rates and lower aggregate SAT scores (Nichols, 2007).

It is difficult to measure the actual outcomes of these studies without complete statistical calculations and individual selection criteria.

This presentation analyzes several quantitative articles and compares statistical methods against research approaches to determine high-stakes testing accuracy and validity.

Reading Curriculum-Based Measurement (R-CBM) standards were used as a basis to determine cut scores and student performance.

The study consisted of a population size of 1,766 students that were followed longitudinally from first through third grades using R-CBM to evaluate student performance.

Several discriminative analysis tools were used to validate testing diagnostic accuracy and validity.

Logistic regression samples with Receiver Operator Characteristic (ROC) curves were conducted to predicate student performance on the R-CBM and National/State required high-stakes tests.

Results suggested that R-CBM is strongly associated with high-stakes testing performance at each grade level and is both accurate and efficient in predicting those students who are likely to pass or fail based on statistical indicators.

With the use of R-CBM educators can predict student performance and identifying students that will pass or fail going all the way back to the first grade (Hintze, 2005).

For the most part this study relied on the following statistical approaches, specificity and negativity, sensitivity, and positive predictive power, respectively.

Discriminate analysis determined the probability outcomes by examining variables describing a population or test group.

Logistic regression techniques use maximum likelihood estimates in which groups are calculated on probability of 0 to100% (Hintze, 2005).

Receiver Operator Characteristic (ROC) curves plot the sensitivity and specificity of a predictor for all possible values of the final cut score (Hintze, 2005).

The R-CBM diagnostic approaches produced consistent and accurate results for predicting performance on high-stakes tests.

Using R-CBM to set cut scores along longitudinal grades resulted in more accurate and efficient method, rather than using a high-stakes test criterion.

The area for concern with R-CBM is with unpredictable changes to the curriculum or composition of the student body, which in turn may skew results on cut scores and will provide a continues moving target.

The question of which statistical approach to use in a school environment to predict cut scores pose a dilemma for educators and policy makers alike (Hintze, 2005).

This certainly creates a difficult situation, and, in many instances, it depends on the expertise and resources of the school district to collect the data (Hintze, 2005).

Educators use Curriculum Based Measurement (CBM) standards for test development and to examine evaluation system for academic performance.

These measurement techniques are used to index student academic performance in the basic skill areas of reading, mathematics, spelling, and written expression (Hintze, 2005).

Educators routinely use CBM standards to monitor individual student progression and instructional effectiveness.

The main feature of CBM is that it provides measurement specifics and evaluation procedures that include testing strategies, administration and scoring of tests, and summarizing results from data collected (Hintze, 2005).

CBM has been proven to be effective in improving curriculum and instruction techniques by use of progressive monitoring techniques along with evaluation check points at each stage of student development.

This study consisted of several different methods to measure a population consisting of 1,766 student participants from seven elementary schools within the same school district.

The data for this experiment were drawn from a set of five groups consisting of first to third grade students longitudinally over 3-year periods (Hintze, 2005).

Initially a total 2,675 students were identified to participate and at first 1,815 qualified thus provided a 69% sample size (Hintze, 2005).

The students were randomly selected for study did not have any major difference in state sponsored testing from the rest of the student population.

The priori power analysis suggested that a sample size this large would provide adequate power (.80) for main effects assuming a small effect size (.10) and an alpha level of .05 (Hintze, 2005).

Specifically, the sample consisted of 49% girls and 51 % boys (Hintze, 2005).

Ethnic breakdown was 3% Native American, 1 % Asian or Pacific Islander, 1% Hispanic, 1% Black not of Hispanic Origin, and 94% White not of Hispanic Origin (Hintze, 2005).

Standard benchmark reading assessment passages consisted of 150 to 250 words in length for first through third grades students were used during the 3- year research project (Hintze, 2005).

The benchmarks reading assessment passages provided adequate evidence of alternate form of reliability that were of relatively equal in difficulty within a grade and increased in difficulty at the higher grades (Hintze, 2005).

Degree of Reading power (DRP) standards were used to develop the reading portion of these exams, with actual DRP scores ranging from 40-56 with an average of 48 on high-stakes tests (Hintze, 2005).

A 5-point scoring rubric evaluated student performances on the reading portion of the standardized test (Hintze, 2005).

The lower rage consisted of scoring rubric levels I, II, and III and the upper end of the scoring rubric consists of levels IV and V which characterize student performance as above grade level proficiency (Hintze, 2005).

Students were required to obtain a median score of 1420 to be considered proficient (Hintze, 2005).

The procedures for this research consisted of eight assessments beginning in the winter of 1st grade and continuing each fall, winter, and spring until the 3rd grade (Hintze, 2005).

The R- CBM exams were administered by qualified and trained staff in accordance with standard administration and scoring procedures.

Likewise, students were administered the reading portion of the state's standardized test in the spring of third grade (Hintze, 2005).

Scores for each of the measures were obtained for all students while all information was consistent and complete to conduct the assessments for the 3-year research period (Hintze, 2005).

To derive research results for this study several different types of statistical data analysis were conducted.

The data was first screened for outliers, distributional properties, and parametric assumptions (Hintze, 2005).

Also, descriptive statistics including correlation findings were inspected that included analysis of R-CBM cut scores that compared three statistical procedures consisting of discriminant analysis, logistic regression, and ROC curves (Hintze, 2005).

ROC allows researchers to model several different cut scores across a variety of assessment situations while the only drawback is that they tend to be subjective.

On the other hand, discriminant analysis and logistic regression both maximize correct classifications using a statistical model.

The extent of these differences may have implications for practice as school-based professionals using R-CBM to predict performance on high-stakes tests (Hintze, 2005).

The data screening procedures for this study examined high-stakes testing scores.

They were examined for accuracy of data entry, missing values, outliers, and conformed to the distributions of multivariate analysis (Hintze, 2005).

Results of the data screening indicated the presence of 49 multivariate outliers as determined through Mahalanobis distance (p <.OO1) with all outliers being deleted (Hintze, 2005).

The descriptive statistics for all assessment measures identify that participants scored on the average above the cut score of 1420 on the reading portion of the state's standardized tests (Hintze, 2005).

The results of the descriptive statistics provided approximately 65% of the sample group passing or meeting minimum proficiency standards while illustrating that R-CBM growth trends within and across grades was quite stable (Hintze, 2005).

The evaluation of distributional properties of earlier R-CBM suggested that the aggregated student performance was positively skewed (Hintze, 2005).

According to Hintze (2005), diagnostic accuracy is addressed by way of a conditional probability analysis that requires a starting diagnostic point in making prediction outcomes.

The proportion outcome is a result of diagnostic accuracy analysis based on sensitivity, specificity, positive predictive power (PPP), and negative predictive power (NPP) (Hintze, 2005).

Sensitivity and specificity provide a way to measure the accuracy of the predictor to identify the presence or absence of a given condition.

Positive and negative predictive powers on the other hand measure efficiency by predicting correctly between who will be identified or not by the criterion measure, once a diagnostic status is known (Hintze, 2005).

The results of the discriminant analysis indicate that using successive R-CBM benchmark assessments as the criterion measure results in consistently higher cut scores as compared to using state high-stakes testing (Hintze, 2005).

The cut scores on the R-CBM ultimately predict performance on state standardized tests; if students do not do well in the R-CBM they usually fail the states standardized exams (Hintze, 2005).

Overall, using R-CBM in a successive manner across grades to ultimately predict performance on the states standardized tests appeared to be a more accurate and efficient approach as compared to the consistent use of the state's criterion.

On a final note, the use of R-CBM is strongly associated with predicting high- stakes testing results.

R-CBM has been proven to be highly effective and efficient in predicting students that will likely pass or fail the high-stakes tests.

This study placed heavy emphasis on specificity and sensitivity with negative/positive predictive power statistics for producing consistent statistical results.

Discriminant analysis determined R-CBM statistical probabilities by examining a variety of approaches along with predictive methods to determine cut scores.

Discriminant R-CBM variables enabled to effectively screen students who were at risk of failing and intervene with improvement measures.

When integrated within preventative program of identification and intervention of failing students, the use of R-CBM will provide educators with an important evaluation and measurement model.

Deploying CBM standards will allows educators with statistical scoring comparisons while providing performance indicators of success and areas for improvement in instruction and curriculum.

Time trend analysis to compare national test averages before and after high-stakes testing policies were also introduced to determine student motivation and achievements (Nichols, 2007).

Across many states that were included in this study it was discovered that high- stakes testing produced an inconsistent effect on student performance (Nichols, 2007).

The research concluded that attaching accountability to statewide tests worked well in some high-stakes states, while it was not an effective policy in all states.

However, the impact of high stakes testing is much lower when it comes to lower grades; as students are conditioned over time, they become more accustomed to test pressures and gain experience to be better test takers (Nichols, 2007).

Several other methods were used to measure the level of pressure of high stakes testing to include rating scales index (1-5), with the highest score reflecting the highest strengths of student accountability (Nichols, 2007).

Indexing scale method did not take into consideration student performance before and after the study period.

Also, a regression model to estimate accountability as a function of how long states had enacted high-stakes testing policy was used to analysis test achievements across Black, Hispanic, and White student groups (Nichols, 2007).

It was discovered that the introduction of state testing accountability had a positive impact on student performance overall.

But when measured by ethnicity, it was found that increases were much lower for Black and Hispanic students than for White students. It was concluded that consequential based policy has a positive impact on achievement for some groups but not others.

However, measure of accountability does not take into consideration state level variations in how accountability policies should be implemented or enforced.

The studies on high-stakes testing did not provide inconclusive evidence that high- stakes testing increases teacher performance and student motivation to learn.

In addition, many of the findings supporting high-stakes testing should be viewed with care since much of the data could be skewed by teachers teaching to the test.

Teachers are given a set of objectives and it makes sense that they will be swayed to prepare students to do well in high-stakes tests and especially since they are being held accountable for the results (Nichols, 2007).

This opens the debate on the effects of high-stakes testing concerning teacher accountability and student motivation and real learning.

It is difficult to conclude high-stakes testing has any systematic and lasting effect on real learning. Evidence suggests that as high-stakes testing determines budgeting criteria for schools the possibility exists for removing low scores and inflating average test results.

Implications for future direction of high-stakes testing hinges on the effective use of statistical process control mechanisms that can be used to make rational decisions and policies based on theory and scientific research.

Time has demonstrated the problems associated with using high-stakes testing; results alone to measure achievement and effectiveness is not working.

Evidence has provided many concerns with the validity of test scores to measure teacher and student performance.

The current system places the burden on teachers to teach to a set of objectives and students to perform at a certain level of proficiency (Nichols, 2007).

It is common knowledge in quality management circles that the workers are blamed many times for the system not operating at full efficiency.

The workers only do what they are instructed to do and it is up to senior management to make sure the system and processes are working as they should while looking for continuous improvement ideas.

Scientific specialists are in the best position to offer any real solutions to the help fix the educational problems to include high stakes testing and any other issues.

They have the background and experience to offer real and lasting solutions based on theory and research.

The authors were dissatisfied with the validity of many of the research approaches because of the inconsistencies and lack of statistical measures used in creating high- stakes testing policies (Nichols, 2007).

The most difficulty to high-stakes testing policies are created by rapid changes in political environments, thus making it difficult to measure and take accurate statistical data (Nichols, 2007).

In addition, every state has adopted some form of high stakes testing and each operates to their own specific needs making it difficult to have consistency or do comparative studies.

The authors also criticize the difficulty to generalize the findings from any one state, district, school, or classroom to another because contextual factors mediate the extent of these effects (Nichols, 2007).

9 Even within states, student and educator perceptions can vary significantly.

Nonetheless, patterns in the data are beginning to emerge that can help us better understand the effects of high stakes testing on public education.

Unfortunately, many of the outcomes of testing have been negative. Certainly, positive effects of testing have been noted; however, people must continually ask whether the benefits outweigh the negative effects.

Any time averaged test results are reported, one must ask the question of who participated in the testing and who did not.

Evidence increasingly suggests that as pressure to perform increases, the lower test scores are more likely to be removed from taking the test therefore inflating average test scores (Nichols, 2007).

Any analysis attempting to connect high stakes testing with achievement must account for the test taking pool.

However, these findings disappeared when the data were disaggregated by the state agencies suggesting that implementation differences probably matter (Nichols, 2007).

States with the same amount pressure may yield increases or decreases in learning, a result that could be attributed to the way the policy is implemented and received (Nichols, 2007).

Implications of high-stakes testing findings resulted in several of the unintended outcomes that in many instances have caused the opposite of the intended use, especially with teachers teaching to the test (Nichols, 2007).

The lack of consistency between states, districts, and counties have caused for disparities between high-stakes testing policies and measurements (Nichols, 2007).

Although high-stakes testing patterns are providing some positive data on effects of high-stakes testing, unfortunately many results have been negative.

People are left out of the decision-making loop while policy makers continue to produce systems that are questionable at best.

The federal governments No-Child-Left-Behind initiative was designed to increase accountability across the board in the educational system by mandating states to implement high-stakes tests.

Many educators and policy makers suggested that teacher and student accountability was the key to improve the educational system in America.

The viewpoint presented by these groups suggested that using test scores to hold teachers accountable was working as intended.

Although the importance of holding teachers accountable can be debatable, it is important to evaluate the intended and unintended outcomes of high-stakes testing.

According to Nichols (2007) some of the unintended outcomes of high-stakes testing, including those related to using tests as a means to hold educators accountable result in the following: effects instruction, effects on student and teacher motivation, and the effects on students who are at-risk of failure.

By examining the evidence presented in this research paper, some unintended outcomes of high-stakes testing have been positive; many of the unintended outcomes have been negative (Nichols, 2007).

Through greater emphases and awareness of the unintended outcomes, school educators and policy makers can work to minimize the negative effects of testing on students.

Research data on the relationship between high stakes testing and its intended purpose of teacher accountability concerning student achievements have been shown to be scattered.

Studies on high-stakes testing have varied in political and social design making it difficult to produce a single strategy that can be measured or studied for the long term.

Politically driven policies have created the biggest stumbling block by continuously changing strategies making it difficult for researchers to replicate earlier analyses.

Several types of statistical methods and processes to describe high-stakes testing performance were used throughout this study.

Educational institutions for example have been perceived to inflate high-stakes testing scores (Nichols, 2007).

This study points out that although testing was proven to be inflated there is very little information on why they occurred in the first place (Nichols, 2007).

Researchers argue that testing inflations can in fact be a statistically natural occurring process.

For example, as teachers and students become more familiar with testing items and objectives testing scores tend to rise in relation to the experience of test taking.

When new and more complex exams are introduced data proves a sharp decline on test scores casting doubt on the analysis of educators purposely manipulating data to inflate testing scores.

High-stakes testing has caused educators and students to focus more on test taking techniques rather than on understanding and learning.

Political policies have placed additional pressures on educators to be evaluated publicly based solely on student test results.

Many states have discovered through various interviews and surveys that high- stakes testing tends to place teachers under pressure to teach to the test (Nichols, 2007).

Although there remains no consensus on the effects of high- stakes testing, studies do provide evidence that further research is needed to explore new and logical improvement initiatives.

Another important study that needs further investigation is the introduction of no- stakes testing, with the intent of comparing the two systems to validate student efficiency and performance (Nichols, 2007).

References

Amrein, A., & Berliner, D. (2003). The Effects of High- Stakes Testing on Student Motivation and Learning.

Educational Leadership, 60(5), 32. Retrieved from Academic Search Complete database.

Berkowitz, B., & Serim, F. (2002). Moving Every Child Ahead: The Big6 Success Strategy. Multimedia

Schools, 9(3), 16. Retrieved from Academic Search Complete database.

Booher-Jennings, J. (2008). Learning to label: Socialization, gender, and the hidden curriculum of high- stakes testing. British Journal of Sociology of Education, 29(2), 149-160. doi:10.1080/01425690701837513.

Borg, M., Plumlee, J., & Stranahan, H. (2007). Plenty of Children Left Behind: High-Stakes Testing and Graduation

Rates in Duval County, Florida. Educational Policy, 21(5), 695- 716. Retrieved from Academic Search Complete database.

Erick, C. (2002). Science Curriculum in Practice: Student Teachers' Use of Hands-On Activities in High- Stakes Testing Schools. NASSP Bulletin, 86(630), 72. Retrieved from Academic Search Complete database.

Jones, B. (2007). The Unintended Outcomes of High-Stakes Testing. Journal of Applied School psychology, 23(2), 65-86. doi:10.1300/J370v23n02_05.

Meyer, L., McClure, J., Walkey, F., Weir, K., & McKenzie, L. (2009). Secondary student motivation orientations and standards-based achievement outcomes. British Journal of Educational Psychology, 79(2), 273-293. Retrieved from Academic Search Complete database.

Nichols, S. (2007). High-Stakes Testing: Does It Increase Achieveme?. Journal of Applied School Psychology, 23(2), 47-64. doi:10.1300/J37nt0v23n02_04.

Sloane, F., & Kelly, A. (2003). Issues in High-Stakes Testing Programs. Theory Into Practice, 42(1), 12. Retrieved from Academic Search Complete database.

Vogler, K., & Virtue, D. (2007). "Just the Facts, Ma'am": Teaching Social Studies in the Era of Standards and High-Stakes Testing. Social Studies, 98(2), 54-58. Retrieved from Academic Search Complete database.

Quasi Experiment Design: Sustained Acceleration of Achievement in reading Comprehension: The New Zealand Experience.

Abstract

This assignment is an article critique of a quasi-experimental design study that was carried out in New Zealand titled "Sustained Acceleration of Achievement in reading Comprehension: The New Zealand Experience." This article investigates low levels of achievement of particularly indigenous and ethnic minorities living in low socioeconomic cities throughout New Zealand. The research consisted of a quasi-experiment design study that was conducted over a period of three years researching and sharing data with several agencies to include schools, government, and researchers. The goal of these organizations was to raise reading comprehension through various strategies of critical discussions, direct student observations, and implementing best practices in the classroom. Through the dedicated efforts of all involved a steady increase in reading comprehension was observed across the period of this experiment. The actual results demonstrate the need for continued testing and collection of data for multiple years to better get a more accurate picture of the reading comprehension programs.

Article Critique Quasi Experiment Design: Sustained Acceleration of Achievement in reading Comprehension: The New Zealand Experience.

This article addresses the importance of adopting effective teaching methods in improving reading comprehension, especially in schools serving culturally and linguistically diverse groups. New Zealand is faced with large disparities in reading comprehension between indigenous and immigrant from many population groups. According to the author, there are two major hypotheses for implementing effective teaching strategies for low performing groups of students living in poor socioeconomic areas. The first strategy draws on data based on best teaching practices and the second relies on collaboration within the teaching community, sharing data and implementing problem solving solutions aimed at improving reading comprehension for socioeconomic disadvantaged students. The goal of these initiatives is aimed at sustaining accelerated rates of improvements in reading comprehension by analyzing the effectiveness of teaching methods and then fine-tuning teaching instruction to better serve the needs of the students.

The reading comprehension initiative was a concerted effort between the schools and the representatives of the New Zealand Ministry of Education. Seven schools with the highest proportion of students from the lowest socioeconomic communities from South Auckland areas were used for this experiment. The experiment concentrated on middle school aged students with school populations ranging from 292 to 593 students. The core data was collected from 14 ethnic groups consisting of over 1,900 students from six schools, with equal male and female representation. Approximately 70 teachers were used per year during for this research study, while two thirds of the teachers had five or more years' experience.

Schools are constantly evolving and dynamically changing, this variability requires specific and deliberate attention that requires longitudinal studies. At its base, this project uses a quasi-experimental design from which qualified judgments are made about possible causal relationships between teaching and learning effectiveness. The quasi-experiment design serves this experiment by testing the effectiveness of the teaching instructions over a period, while allowing for the properties of variability. Several repeated measures of students reading comprehension scores were collected at six different times as part of quasi-experiment design. The quasi-experiment design consisted of a single-case logic technique as a development framework of cross-sectional and longitudinal data gathered at different stages of this project aimed at improving reading comprehension for low socioeconomic students. The first phase consisted of a planned intervention initiative analyzing and discussing of data. The second phase consisted of developing instructional practices through workshops and the third phase involved sustainability to continuously improve the reading comprehension program.

The methods of measurements for reading comprehension were collected using the Progressive Achievement Tests (PAT). The PAT test serves as standardized method to repeatedly measure students' progression and allow for comparison of student reading comprehension performance across several schools. For reliability of the data the researchers developed interschool standardized process of administering the exams and moderating the accuracy of teacher scoring. The instructional portion of the program involved observation of reading sessions from classrooms under observation. The initial observations involved tape recordings of the reading sessions and the subsequent observations involved systematic video transcripts of 15 classroom lessons. Data analysis used in this experiment consisted of repeated measures using raw scores and normalized scores over the course of this research. Standard statistical tests for mean differences were used such as Hotelling T2 tests, chi-square tests, and effect sizes Cohen's d test, and multivariate analysis of variance test. At the start of this experiment the PAT exams indicated the average student had trouble on the reading comprehension portion of the exam. The student under observation scored below the average in the range of 3.10, indicating that over 60% of the students were two years below reading comprehension levels.

This research challenged the school system in New Zealand for implementation of more effective teaching strategies, specifically aimed at improving the reading comprehension of socioeconomic disadvantaged students. Although the data suggests that gains have been made in improving reading comprehension for minority students, the fact remains that large disparities remain.

The proposed research consisted of collaboration and changes within the teaching instructional methods, producing the most effective solutions for presenting lessons in reading comprehension. These components were implemented in three phases within a network of seven schools. The quasi-experimental design with its in-built replication and comparison provided evidence to support the claim that improvements in the reading comprehension program were because of intervention at all stages of the learning process. This study provides further evidence that effective instruction is a result of best practices of teaching and learning methods based on a systematic collection of data, analysis, and discussion. These essential elements of teaching process improvement initiatives provide the environment for success of culturally and linguistic diverse students.

References

Mei Kuin, L., McNaughton, S., Amituanai-Toloa, M., Turner, R., & Hsiao, S. (2009). Sustained Acceleration of Achievement in Reading Comprehension: The New Zealand Experience. Reading Research Quarterly, 44(1), 30-56. Retrieved from EBSCOhost.

Causal-Comparative Research: A Comparison of Urban Teacher Characteristics for Student

Interns Placed in Different Urban School Settings

Abstract

This assignment requires the critique of an of a casual comparative research article. This research article examines the difference of urban teacher characteristics between interns placed in urban professional development schools and non-professional school environment. Several urban universities worked in partnership for this experiment to investigate student intern characteristics in different settings. Teachers were selected to take part of an interview process to asses' characteristics that included the following: persistence, values, action in implementing ideas, approach towards at-risk students, orientation procedures, dealing with bureaucracy, fallibility, success of teachers and students, and planning and organizing. The students were given assessments before and after the internship experience. The casual comparative research design included a pre-and-post-test that was compared using descriptive statistics and Analysis of Covariance statistical procedures. This experiment concluded that there was no statistical difference between the two groups, although there were individual instances of growth and decline in each of the characteristics measured. This experiment could not conclusively link the initiatives of professional development program in improving urban teacher characteristics.

A Comparison of Urban Teacher Characteristics for Student Interns Placed in Different

Urban School Settings

Majority believe that there is room for improvements in the educational system in America and especially in urban districts. At the root, many issues effecting urban school districts are characteristics of poor instruction and deficiencies in teacher recruitment and retention. It is believed that to better serve these urban communities it is important to develop professional educators that are committed to making a difference in the lives of students. Research suggests that successful urban teachers possess several characteristics that involve not only the classroom but outside activities in the community. Urban school districts have taken the initiative to develop specific programs to address the development of teachers by creating the professional development schools. This program is aimed at developing student intern, beginning teachers, along with looking at ways to improvement the experienced pool of teachers.

This research examined urban professional development school programs and how they contributed to the quality of instruction and growth of teacher's characteristics. The participants in this study were comprised of student interns from two urban universities involving seven professional development school sites. The professional development program was designed to prepare 59 student interns for urban settings while allowing the students to either, enroll in the professional or the non-professional development program. From this group, 29 student interns completed the professional development school and were compared to non-professional development school student interns. Considering the variables of demographics and teaching experience each student candidate was required to master similar requirements.

All student interns were given the Urban Teacher Selection Interview assessments before and after completion of training period. Student interns were also given final assessments during the last internship training seminar at the last week of the training. The Urban Teacher Selection Interview assessments played an important part in measuring student intern development of the 10 effective urban teacher characteristics that included the following: Persistence, Values Children's Learning, and Theory to Practice, Work with At-Risk Students, Approach to Children, The Bureaucracy, Admit Mistakes, Teacher Success, Student Success, and Planning/Organization. A key fact to remember is that only one out ten undergraduates passes the Urban Teacher Selection Interview assessments.

The data collected from the Urban Teacher Selection Interview assessments were analyzed using descriptive statistics and analysis of covariance. The mean scores for both student interns in the urban professional development school and urban nonprofessional development school were notably similar, with mean score averages of 43. The student interns placed in an urban professional development school increased the most in the characteristics of planning/organization and decreased in work with at-risk students. The final posttest scores showed that 75.9% of the urban professional development school student interns and 86.7% of the urban non-professional development school student interns received a low rating on these characteristics.

The analysis of covariance performed on the post-test scores of the Urban Teacher Selection Interview assessments revealed the difference between the two groups at the .05 level of significance. The results demonstrate that the short-term training may not be adequate to properly train student intern teachers in the urban school environment.

The findings suggest that the efforts of the professional development school initiative to build the required characteristics in teaching in urban environments could not be established as noted in the Urban Teacher Selection Interview assessments. Although the statistics revealed that the professional development school program was not as effective as thought of, it does serve as a worthwhile endeavor. Further study may be required with larger populations sample sizes to increase the generalization of the findings.

References

Robinson, J., McKinney, S. E., & Spooner, M. (2004). A Comparison of Urban Teacher Characteristics for Student Interns Placed in Different Urban School Settings. Professional Educator, 26(2), 17-30. Retrieved from EBSCO host.

Correlational Research: The school shooting/violent video game link: causal relationship or moral panic?

Abstract

In the last decade school violence has reached new heights with multiple homicides at several campuses in America and different parts of the world. This trend has placed much attention on finding out the root causes for school shootings and aggressive behavior in schools, placing violent video games on the spotlight as the potential cause. Many researchers have attempted to make comparisons between laboratory and correlation research on school shooting incidences and relating them to violent video games.

This research paper takes the position that many claims against video games as being the culprit behind the rise in school shootings as simply false and is not backed up by scientific data to support their claims. Researchers on both sides continue to be significantly divided in methodology to investigate the correlation between video game research and increase in school violence. This research paper concluded that the data does not support the theory of linking a relationship between school shooting incidents and violent video games.

The school shooting/violent video game link: causal relationship or moral panic?

The Virginia Tech school massacre in 1997 brought about much debate regarding the influence of violent video games and other forms of violent media for fueling school shootings. Many so-called experts in mainstream media have blamed these increases in school aggression and violence on violent video games and the gaming industry. Many suggest that these acts of homicide were conducted by young males because of their exposure to violent video games. Investigators were much surprised to discover that many of these individuals that committed these violent school shootings had very little exposure to violent video games. In the other hand, in the Columbine High shooting the perpetrators were known to be avid players of violent video games. The debate continues with much speculation that is not backed by research or data to support many of the claims that violent video games are the culprit to school shootings. This research paper will attempt to bridge this gap between facts and speculation that continues to be hotly debated in the media.

The speculation concerning the relationship between violent video games and school shootings are not only limited to the media, many scholars have also attempted to link the two. One must question the basis for the generalization of these conclusions so called expert researchers.

The research concerning violent video games thus falls into two categories, experimental and correlation. In the experimental design for example students are exposed to either to games that are, or not violent while being observed for aggressive behavior. The issue of examining aggression in laboratory settings proves to be constrained and does apply to actual real-world physical acts of aggression.

These research studies have proved to be mixed; some support and others do not support their findings linking violent video games to school shootings. Correlational research on the other hand is considered to produce weaker results than experimental research. Correlational results are also mixed with some studies finding the relationship and others not finding any linkage at all between violent video games and school shootings and increased aggression. The major pitfall of correlational research is that it does not take into consideration environmental factors and physical conditions such as personality and genetics.

Given that the data on school shooters is based on a very small population of individuals it is difficult to specifically relate these violent behaviors to one factor. This limited sample size creates difficulty for researchers to statistically produce results based on empirical research. Using approaches of threat and risk assessments can include profiling of school shooters while using caution in over identifying or falsely interpreting the data.

That the data collected from the small sample of school shooters identifying their delinquencies and aggression may not prove or predict future acts of school violence. The Department of Education and secret service conducted the most comprehensive study on school shooters involved 41 perpetrators.

The secret service concluded that school shooters were diverse, and it would be very difficult to identify or predict threats in advance. The secret service also identified that only 59% of the perpetrators demonstrated some interest in violent media of any kind.

Nonetheless, the evidence available on school shooters does not support the hypothesis that violent video games play a role in instigating of school shootings. There seems to be a lack of high-quality evidence to support the predictive results and risk factors associated with linking violent video games to school shootings or increased aggression.

The significant spread of pinpointing the root causes of these violent individuals is inherently varied that include multiple risk factors that must be considered in whole. Setting aside individuals that claim a violent act in advance there is not enough data that exists to profile potential school shooters without significant false alarms. This review of violent video games and school shootings serves as a platform for further debate and research and as a potential for public awareness and policy.

References

Ferguson, C. J. (2008). The school shooting/violent video game link: causal relationship or moral panic? Journal of Investigative Psychology & Offender Profiling, 5(1/2), 25-37. Retrieved from EBSCO host.

News Article Review Week 1: Brave New Schools, District's Ban on Religious Speech Ordered to Trial

Legal Team Notes Rules Adopted in Attempt to Criminalize Christianity

Brave New Schools, District's Ban on Religious Speech Ordered to Trial, Legal Team Notes

Rules Adopted in Attempt to Criminalize Christianity

The article titled "Brave New Schools" describes a Florida school district attempts at banning freedom of religious speech. An organization dedicated to advancing religious freedom has been fighting this school district in Florida for several years. A federal judge has ordered a trial concerning the school districts restrictions of religious speech policies. Mathew Staver, founder of the Liberty Counsel, commented "School employees do not lose their constitutional rights as a precondition to receiving a government paycheck."

The American Civil Liberties Union (ACLU) initiated the Consent Decree adopted by the Santa Rosa County, Florida School Board. The Consent Decree resulted from an earlier lawsuit prompting by complaints that adults were praying at optional and sponsored off-campus events. The Liberty Counsel claims that the Consent Decree adopted by the Santa Rosa school district is "blatantly unconstitutional and in fact an attempt at criminalizing Christianity." The Liberty Counsel has brought legal challenge a few months ago giving a "Notice of Potentially Improper or Unethical Conduct" requesting an investigation against a new principle in the school district. The ACLU and the school district managers have requested the case to be dismissed. The trail is expected this summer and the judge overseeing this case has ordered the school board not to enforce any school policies that restrain employee's participation in speeches or in private religious service.

The real question in this news story should read more like, what are the Florida school district and ACLU afraid of? Are they so deeply concerned that they would lose control over their teachers and students alike, if they believed in the higher authority of God? This was the chief reason the founding fathers of America risked their lives for, to break away from the shackles of the King of England and his tyranny over all aspects of society in the new world. John Adams and John Hancock said, "We recognize no sovereign but God, and no King but Jesus," supporting the thoughts and minds of early American leaders such as Thomas Jefferson and Benjamin Franklin and many others.

History has many examples, were information was controlled and the news was based purely on propaganda and misinformation. Most are aware of the consequences of limiting freedom of speech; communism, socialism, and fascism systems that control and manipulate all aspects of life by manipulative strategies of brainwashing the public. A great case can be made for faith-based education; religion teaches us morals and the consequences of not obeying Gods commands are bleak.

Faith based education would help place morality on the forefront; the fact is that we have a multicultural society and we have a mixture of believers and non-believers to include several different religious groups. Offering Bible study to include the Old and New Testaments in the school's curriculum especially to the younger generations would make the biggest impact in instilling morality and decency that is lacking today. It is dangerous not to offer people with choices and exposure too many forms of education to include faith-based teachings. It is important for people to have access to all forms of information and they should make up their minds on their own and not by special interest groups such as the ACLU.

References

Bob Unruh (2011), Brave New Schools, District's ban on religious speech ordered to trial, Legal team notes rules adopted in attempt to criminalize Christianity, World Net Daily, Retrieved from http://www.wnd.com/index.php?fa=PAGE.view&pageId=278021

School Reverses Course and Allows Students to Post Ten Commandments on Lockers

School Reverses Course and Allows Students to Post Ten Commandments on Lockers

The council recently praised the Floyd County High School administration to allow students to display the Ten Commandments on the front of their lockers. The posting of the Ten Commandments was in direct support of the students at neighboring Giles County High School, where the school administrators banned the display of the Ten Commandments on school lockers after lawsuit threats. Members of the Fellowship of Christian Athletes placed copies of the Ten Commandments on the face of their individual lockers. Shortly after, the Floyd County High School administrators personally removed the postings of the Ten Commandments from the lockers.

The council took immediate action and notified the high school to reverse their decision and allow for religious material or face a federal lawsuit. The school officials finally allowed the students to post the Ten Commandments on their individual lockers. The school officials could in fact ban any type of posting on the face of the lockers but could not discriminate against religious viewpoints while allowing for others.

America was founded on religious principles and particularly in Christianity, the founding fathers echoed the words, "America is a Christian Nation." The last two or three decades the American solid foundation of being a Christian Nation is being placed to the test, with opposing groups trying to push their own agendas. All the nations of the world to include the many other major religious groups look up to the Godly shining beacon America represents; were people are free from tyranny and are free to practice their religion, with a republic form of government where the leaders are chosen by the people. The strategy of removing religion and

God from society serves the puppet masters well in being able to manipulate and control the masses. Plato said, "One of the penalties for refusing to participate in politics is that you end up being governed by your inferiors." Important lesson can be taken by Plato's wisdom; the students at Floyd County High School should be applauded for standing up for their faith and supporting the solid religious foundation in which American republic was founded on, a Christian Nation.

References

Liberty Counsel, March 10, 201, School Reverses Course and Allows Students to Post Ten Commandments on Lockers, retrieved from,
http://lc.org/index.cfm?PID=14100&PRID=1043

Interfaith Initiative Formed for Colleges

Interfaith Initiative Formed for Colleges

The White House recently released an announcement for a new initiative to encourage college students of different religion to work together on a yearlong community service project. Colleges throughout America will be asked to participate in this program titled, The Presidents Interfaith and Community Service Campus Challenge" for the 2011-2012 academic school calendar. The purpose of this initiative is to encourage cooperation amongst students of different faith, to include non-believers.

In Genesis, the Bible recounts that all mankind are decedents of Adam; reminding us that we all have roots to one blood line. The Bible is full of stories of acceptance of others and many instances of enemies being embraced in peace. In Exodus the Hebrews are reminded what it was like to be strangers in foreign lands. By casting out others of different faith, thought, and ideals we lose the potential of their wisdom and knowledge that can be gained in improving the daily lives of all. The major benefit of accepting others is the opportunity to share the teachings of the Scriptures and the gospels of our Lord. One of the greatest commandments of Jesus was to love your neighbor.

In Mathew 5:43 it states, "You have heard that it was said, "You shall love your neighbor and hate your enemy. But I say to you, love your enemies, bless those who curse you, do good to those who hate you, and pray for those who spitefully use you and persecute you, that you may be sons of your Father in heaven; for He makes His sun rise o the evil and on the good, and sends rain on the just and on the unjust." God warns us that He is the ultimate authority and no man should be judge or jury on any other man, for all there is no human is without sin.

References

Laurie Goodstein, (2011), Interfaith Initiative Formed for Colleges, Published: March 17, 2011, Retrieved from, http://www.nytimes.com/2011/03/18/us/politics/18brfs-INTERFAITHIN_BRF.html?_r=1&ref=education

John C. Maxwell, 2007, The Maxwell Leadership Bible, Lessons in Leadership from the Word of God, Second Edition

Many Ways and Reasons to Cheat on Tests

Many Ways and Reasons to Cheat on Tests

This article examines educational high-stakes testing policies as they relate to teacher accountability and specifically highlighting the unethical behavior of many teachers. For example, "in an Arizona State University survey published last year, more than 50% of teachers and other educators admitted to some kind of cheating on Arizona's state tests" (Upton, 2011). The online survey to define cheating consisted of over 3,000 educators, with cheating broadly defined by accidently leaving score sheets in the classroom to be changing answers on score sheets (Upton, 2011).

High-stakes testing policies have triggered much debate and much further studies need to be conducted to examine why so many teachers are compromising the high-stakes exams and whether its promise to increase student learning has been fulfilled. The consequences of cheating on high-stakes tests can be drastic and result in higher administration costs in retesting and other psychological effects on students that are difficult to measure, especially in the lower grades (Upton, 2011).

The federal governments No-Child-Left-Behind program was designed to increase accountability across the board in the U.S. educational system, by mandating states to implement high-stakes tests. By examining the evidence presented in this article many unintended outcomes of high-stakes testing have been negative. Through greater emphases and awareness of the unintended outcomes, school educators and policy makers can work to minimize the negative effects of the high-stakes testing programs.

Political policies have placed additional pressures on educators to be evaluated publicly based solely on student high-stakes test results. Many states have discovered through various interviews and surveys that high-stakes testing tends to place teachers under pressure to teach to the test and or flat out cheat. Although there remains no consensus on the effects of high-stakes testing, studies do provide evidence that further research is needed to explore new and logical improvement initiatives. According to Maxwell (2007)

"Ethics cannot be categorized in our lives. People try to use one set of ethics for their professional life, another for their spiritual life and still another at home with their family. This gets them in trouble, ethics is ethics" (p.641). It is apparent that many educators do not agree with federally mandated high-stakes testing, but the fact remains educators must uphold the highest ethical standards.

References

Jodi Upton, Denise Amos and Anne Ryman, USA TODAY, Updated 3/10/2011
http://www.usatoday.com/news/education/2011-03-10-

1Aschooltesting10_CV_N.htm?loc=interstitialskip

John C. Maxwell, 2007, The Maxwell Leadership Bible, Lessons in Leadership from the Word of God, Second Edition

Character and Academics: What Good Schools Do

Character and Academics: What Good Schools Do

This article emphasizes the importance of character and the traits important that are directly linked to leadership that includes selflessness, decisiveness, energy, commitment, loyalty, and integrity. Good leaders have these personality characteristics of emotional stability, enthusiasm, conscientiousness, tough-mindedness, and self-assurance based on a foundation of faith.

The author also discusses the importance of developing programs to teach character in the classroom. Also, it describes different initiatives taken from several schools and programs involving community service and other group activities. Strong moral character is what followers expect and look for in a good leader.

Character is something you gain from an early age and is influenced by your family, friends, and environmental conditions. Most of us are born with a sound mind and we intrinsically know from right and wrong, when you look at it really comes down to making the right conscience choice. It is reasonable to assume that certain character and personality traits are associated with leadership, while others are not.

Many times, we focus on character and leadership traits associated with success, but it is interesting to understand failures of leadership as well. Some leaders forget about the goal and concentrate on themselves instead of the whole. Negative characteristic traits that can affect leadership consist of selfishness, meaning that we concentrate on our needs and not the good of others. As a leader will you choose the route of least resistance or will you make the right decision based on traits of integrity, honesty, and courage in sync with the teachings of the Scriptures?

References

Benninga, J. S., Berkowitz, M. W., Kuehn, P., & Smith, K. (2006). Character and Academics: What Good Schools Do. Phi Delta Kappan, 87(6), 448-452. Retrieved from EBSCOhost.

SOCIAL RESPONSIBILITY

Social responsibility in the classroom means to be a responsible and respectful individual; demonstrating common courtesy towards others by listening to what they have to say and being silent as they speak. Respect is a two-way street, as a leader you must show respect up and down the chain of command. Social responsibility of a leader should be directly related to the goal and common good of the team. My goal for this class was to create a collaborative and non-confrontational environment between myself and the team. Everyone one in my team was professional in every sense of the word.

COMMITMENT / WORK ETHIC

University intensives were exhausting, especially when completing two back-to-back courses. The only recommendation I would have is shorten the amount of time for group presentations and allowing more discussions in the classroom. In this class, I was fortunate not to have a dominating type of personality in the group, everyone worked in sync and harmony with each other. We all put in many hours of work into completing a professional and efficient product. I tactfully included ideas and information to the team and assisted as much as possible by providing examples and different ideas.

REFLECTION

Reflecting to the last two weeks at University, I must say that the overall experience has been great, and I enjoyed meeting my fellow students and faculty alike. Because of my personality, I do take a while to get to know people and open and especially faculty. University is a first-class organization that not only teaches traditional subjects but integrates the scriptures and I am thankful to study the Word of God. I would recommend university to anyone I encounter and praise the faculty and administration for an outstanding job.

INTEGRITY

Leadership is about having integrity and a total commitment to the highest personal ethical standards. As a proven leader I feel that my actions speak for themselves and during this course my main concern was always towards the wellbeing of my team members. I do on many occasions speak out, but my intentions are good, and I try to get to the point by being honest and truthful with my feedback. Integrity, to a good leader means to have backbone and stand up for people under your command. I recognize the importance of integrity and without it everything is lost, respect, loyalty, and commitment.

PROFESSIONALISM

Professionalism can be characterized by a set of values and characteristics that describe individual actions towards the betterment of society. Professionals are held to a higher set of standards and have an obligation in contributing their efforts towards the service of others.

After serving for over 20 years in the US Air Force may qualify me as a professional, placing duty and country above all. My team members were outstanding citizens and professionals that have devoted most of their lives towards

the betterment of education in society. I am grateful towards
my team members for their commitment and help in
completing the final team project.

Effective executive: The definitive guide to getting the right things done.

Effective executive: The definitive guide to getting the right things done.

A willingness to get the right things done is what good executives do; they must have the self-confidence to make timely and wise decisions (Drucker, 2006). The executive is also required to effectively communicate his/her decision to their subordinates and board members. In most corporations a moment arrives when brave decisions must be made if an enterprise is to be carried through.

Decisiveness includes the willingness to accept responsibility. Leaders are always accountable, and this includes when things go right and when things go wrong. The executive provides the overall strategic planning for the organization while promoting cooperation and teamwork with a vision towards mission accomplishment.

Successful executives realize it is extremely difficult to control their time or the people around them (Drucker, 2006). The most important thing to realize as an executive is to remain flexible and adjust fit the situation or task at hand. Executives are always faced with making hard decisions; the choice depends on each individual executive to choose between the route of least resistance or the right decision based on strong leadership characteristics of integrity, honesty, and courage.

The ability of executive to make the right and sound decisions is what separates them from their peers, while in the process gaining the respect of their subordinates. Executives also realize it is extremely difficult to control or change people around them. Sure, they can easily use their position power and authority, but this would not be true leadership. True leadership is displayed while an executive turns his/her back on their people and they in-turn do the right thing, because they want to and not because they were order to.

Successful executives realize they must continuously to adjust their decision-making process to fit the situation at hand.

Intrinsic motivation comes from internal factors that are within an individual while being motivated by goal or task placed ahead. On the other hand, extrinsic motivations are external factors that come in the form of reward and punishment that are outside the individual control.

These motivation techniques are just part of the tools used by effective executives in managing their operations. Executives need to have a breath of education and experience in the areas of leadership, management, and psychology to include personality typing to be more effective at their position. We all have different personalities and the most effective executives realize this and change their style of leading to fit the situation.

Executives realize the importance of delegating and they accomplish this by allowing their subordinates to make decisions at the lowest levels while providing for flexibility for them to oversee their own affairs. Allowing subordinates to take charge of their tasks gives them a sense of empowerment and self-responsibility (Drucker, 2006).

This allows executives to have more time on strategic planning and less on day-today managing of personnel. Most individuals want to do a good job, and, in many instances, it is the executives that fail their people. Executives influence people by leading by good example, successful executives get out behind their desk and visit their people on the floor or work environment.

Looking back at the trends of human energy output in the last two centuries; the transition from human labor energy output compared to machines provides a blueprint for the future (Drucker, 2006). Machines have surpassed energy produced by humans by thousands fold. Technology and machines have produced an abundance never witnessed before in human history; with this continual trend the human physical workforce will eventually diminish completely.

Most corporations are concerned with their bottom line and profit gains while the only way they can achieve this is through automation and less employees. Soon will not need people to do mundane brainless tasks; we will need innovative and highly trained people in the sciences and technology to develop better and smarter systems.

References

Drucker, P.F. (2006). The effective executive: The definitive guide to getting the right things done. New York, NY: Harper Collins.

Professional Integrity Competence and Integrity

If you could describe educational leaders with one word it would be "Professional," to be a professional you must be committed towards the betterment of society on whole. Professional fully describes an educational leader, because majority of teachers serve most of their adult lifetime in their positions serving others. Teachers are considered professionals through their actions as demonstrated by self-sacrifice, devotion, and passion towards education and their student's well-being.

An educational leader must possess the highest ethical standards and personal characteristics to be effective in their day-to-day activities. The foundation of an educational professional is based on leadership traits that consist of integrity, loyalty, honesty, and a commitment towards mission accomplishment. Integrity means to be above reproach with an unwavering character to stay true to the cause. Character based on high ethical standards is what makes an educational leader respected by their superiors, peers, community, and their students.

Educational leaders are entrusted with teaching and serve as role models for their students. Responsibility to raise children right not only falls on the shoulders of educators but to parents and community leaders and they all must be active partners in the education of their children.

Decision Making Essay

Our group consisted of individuals with varied professional backgrounds and the one leadership trait that stands out about my team members is character. They all had a sense of professionalism along with sound leadership traits based on character, integrity, and honesty. These same leadership traits were displayed during the entire process of completing the group assignment and presentation. The smooth and cooperative efforts of all team members were evident; no one team member was overbearing or had to have it his or her way and this led towards synergy within the group. The first step of the decision-making process was the planning stage; on the first day we discussed the entire case study and investigated the school's strategic plans and the environment of the school and the community.

The second step was to identify the root problems and offer several solutions. The third step was to agree upon two criteria and provide detailed plans for implementation. The final step was to present our findings to the school district and allow for open debate and discussion. Our efforts provided a road map towards securing the school environment, while placing emphasis in retaining qualified teachers using the SWAT analysis template.

Personal Professional Development Plan of Action

Professionals serving in any capacity have an obligation towards seeking further education and continuously improving in the way they lead and manage their day-to-day activities and their lives. My world view was mostly impacted during my service of over 20 year's active duty in the U.S. Air Force.

This experience helped hone my leadership skills through many years of trial and error coupled with continues education and training. I was also fortunate to have studied about Dr W. Edwards Deming and his philosophy on life in general along with his famous Total Quality Management (14 Point) theories. Dr Deming provides leaders and managers with a wealth of information and ideas to work smarter based on a never-ending cyclical process of continues improvement.

The second most important tool a good leader should possess is the ability to understand people using various personality profiling techniques. Understanding your people and being aware of one's capabilities and limitations may determine success or failure of a leader in many circumstances. Educational leaders should attend professional conferences and seminars if time and funds are available.

With today's financial constraints many organizations are turning towards online seminars and training programs to save funds and time. Along with training seminars there are many self-improvement books and magazines that are specific in nature and may fit in the overall scheme of improving leadership and management capabilities of an educational leader.

The World Wide Web is a rich source of information that provides an overabundance of information and the capability to join social and professional organizations online. Today educational leaders have access to many resources to share and collaborate with their professional peers exchanging ideas and best practices.

References

Dr. L M Foong (2011) SWOT Analysis Template, Retrieved from: http://swotanalysistemplate.com/

The W. Edwards Deming Institute (2011) The Deming System of Profound Knowledge

Retrieved from: http://deming.org/index.cfm?content=66

Effective executive: Guide to getting the right things done.

Solomon said an individual does not have any control over the timing of most events and the best one can do is recognize the timing of the event. The foundation of an executive's effectiveness hinges on recording of time, managing time, and consolidating time (Drucker, 2006). Leaders in executive positions at best can only attempt to manage their time because internal and external events dictate on what and were an executive's time is spent.

It would be easy to compare the role of an executive to a firefighter; just as a fire fighters' job is to distinguish a fire, an executive diffuses organizational events before they get out of control. Recording and tracking of time helps executives better manage their day-to-day activities. Executives are left with very little choice but to block a few hours a day to complete special reports or projects which cannot be delegated (Drucker, 2006).

Successful executives realize that power does not come from their position, but the ability to effectively delegate as much as possible to free their time for higher impact organizational tasks (Drucker, 2006). A major responsibility of an executive is to groom individuals under their command and control. To develop their people, an executive must delegate responsibilities and empower individuals to be able to think and act on their own. By empowering people, an executive is in fact distributing work and more effectively managing his/her time, while allowing for better collaboration and teamwork within and other departments throughout the organization.

Executives are responsible for the overall strategic planning of the organization and are obligated to promote cooperation and teamwork with a vision towards mission accomplishment. The organizational executive is responsible for creating the framework by which personnel interact with each other in implementing the goals within their environment. It is important that the executive promotes a positive and nurturing culture which recognizes excellence and identifies improvement areas within an organization.

Executives who record and analyze their time more effectively tend to be more mission oriented. Time management allows executives to focus their efforts on the most important goals which contribute to the growth of the organization. Executives must be discretionary with their time to concentrate on the most mission critical tasks. For example, when Moses freed the Israelites from Egypt, he quickly learned the difficulty of providing for the masses. He simply did not enough time in the day to handle all the personnel issues of his people.

With his father in-law's guidance, Moses learned the basic principles of delegation. Moses quickly delegated majority of his duties to his most trusted judges, thus freeing him from mundane tasks and allowed him to concentrate on the most sever duties. Executives are also confronted by the daily demands of their duties, the demands of their people, and the demands of time and change and innovation (Drucker, 2006).

Effective executives know transformation of management is obtained through application of time management techniques and knowledge. Change for the sake of attempting new ideas are simply not enough, it must take an all-out effort of transformation and effective application of the strategy. Executives work diligently at managing where and how their time is used, while concentrating on their major objectives and goals (Drucker, 2006). Effective executives force themselves to concentrate on their priorities, accomplishing the most mission critical tasks first. Executive effectives can be measured by how well they manage their time, while placing the needs of their people and mission above personnel ambitions.

References

Drucker, P.F. (2006). The effective executive: The definitive guide to getting the right things done. New York, NY: Harper Collins.